ORGANIZING WOMEN OFFICE WORKERS

Dissatisfaction, Consciousness, and Action

Roberta Goldberg

PRAEGER

PRAEGER SPECIAL STUDIES • PRAEGER SCIENTIFIC

Library of Congress Cataloging in Publication Data

Goldberg, Roberta.
  Organizing women office workers.

  Originally presented as the author's thesis
(American University)
  Bibliography: p.
  Includes index.
  1. Baltimore Working Women (Organization)
2. Women clerks—Maryland—Baltimore—Case studies.
3. Job satisfaction—Maryland—Baltimore—Case
studies. I. Title.
HD6073.M392U525   1983   331.88′116513′097526   82-18907

ISBN 0-03-063287-0

Published in 1983 by Praeger Publishers
CBS Educational and Professional Publishing
a Division of CBS Inc.
521 Fifth Avenue, New York, New York 10175 U.S.A.

© 1983 Praeger Publishers

Printed in the United States of America

For my parents,
who provided the foundation
with love.

Acknowledgments

As with any work that requires most of one's energy for an extended period of time, I have many people to thank for their ideas and support. I am most indebted to the members and staff of Baltimore Working Women who generously opened their doors to me, supplied crucial information, and supported my work with enthusiasm and trust. Much of what I learned from these women is not measurable or accountable in the context of a research project such as this—their courage and strength are an ongoing source of inspiration. My contacts with Working Women, National Association of Office Workers were also of great value, and I thank everyone in both the national organization and in Baltimore for their support and help.

Two fellowships have assisted me in the research and preparation of this book. The American University Dissertation Fellowship and the Lena Lake Forrest Fellowship from the Business and Professional Women's Foundation provided much needed funding at crucial steps along the way.

I am also greatly indebted to Jo Thornton for her typing skill, editorial knowledge, and patience. Her talents are a strong reminder of the importance of office work.

Among those who have advised me along the way, I am especially grateful to the members of my dissertation committee, Muriel Cantor, Ken Kusterer, and Jurg Siegenthaler, for their helpful comments and suggestions. Their interest in my work from its inception has been invaluable. I would like to thank Mr. Ki Whang Kim who through his wisdom has instilled in me the patience and discipline necessary to complete this project. The following colleagues and friends have also been supportive throughout, both academically and personally: Louise Arts, Sarah Berger, Joon P. Choi, Joe Cuevas, Jan Houbolt, Roxana Moayede, Larry Riley, Gail Rothberg, Marc Silver, Susan Soucek, Bobbie Spalter-Roth, and Sadie White. Each of them has made a special contribution that I will always remember.

Contents

Chapter 1

Introduction

This study is an examination of the concepts of dissatisfaction and consciousness as they were experienced by women office workers who belong to a working women's organization. While there have been studies of the history of women workers and how they fit into the occupational and social structure,[1] little attention has been paid to the worker herself or to the problems she encounters on the job.[2] Consequently, we have little information to help us understand how or why the recent workers' movement has arisen. This study focuses on the process by which women have become aware of their own dissatisfaction as workers, and to what extent they see this as tied to their specific jobs and/or the fact that they are women.

In order to pursue this issue, I conducted a case study of one organization, Baltimore Working Women, that is part of the working women's movement. I have concentrated on the dissatisfactions that the women experience at work and the consciousness that prevails as they participate in this office workers' organization. I also investigated their work experiences and other relevant information pertaining to the participants. Included in this study is an examination of the origins and history of the group itself, its present structure, an overview of the issues raised by its members, and strategies for action.

In essence, I investigated the types of consciousness that women in clerical work roles experience in relation to class and gender as they participate in working women's organizations. These findings help clarify the unique conditions for women who experience specific demands in terms of family obligations and at the same time must work for wages outside the home. With many women entering the work force today, we can assume there will be changes in the family and in the society as sex-based responsibilities are altered. Such changes will affect how women view themselves and their relationships to their work obligations.[3] At the same time, there have been profound changes in the workplace due to economic and technological changes.[4] The availability of large numbers of women to work in the fastest-growing, labor-intensive fields is tied to undesirable working conditions, and thus to their dissatisfaction as workers.

There were two central questions to which this research was directed.

1. *What are the specific types of dissatisfaction found among women office workers?*

Dissatisfaction is defined as the conditions of the work experience and environment that the worker finds undesirable or unacceptable. It may be expressed in a number of direct or indirect (and in some cases even unconscious) behavior patterns. The specific causes of dissatisfaction and the responses to it will be described in the following chapters by the women interviewed, as well as in the relevant literature. Dissatisfaction with pay, absence of, or inadequate job descriptions, assuring legal rights, and job security are among the most frequently raised issues. The primary source of information is an extensive analysis of office workers' own thoughts on this subject. This approach provides unique insight into specific causes of worker dissatisfaction.

2. *What types of consciousness exist among women who participate in office workers' organizations?*

Three types of consciousness are delineated in this study:

a. Job consciousness involves an identification with others in the same occupational situation, for instance, all office workers, and a recognition that they share several important concerns such as job security and wages.[5] Consciousness on this level does not go beyond the job setting. Conceptually, it is useful in understanding a particular practical level of awareness on the part of workers.

b. Feminist consciousness involves an awareness of the subordinate position of women in various areas of the social structure. The workplace and the family are the two most relevant areas for the purposes of this research, although consciousness in these areas can overlap with others such as education, the legal system, and sexuality. A woman's awareness is defined as feminist if she believes her dissatisfaction with work and her family status is due at least in part to the fact that she is female.[6]

Job consciousness and feminist consciousness are clearly related and, to a significant extent, inseparable. Since so much of a woman's work life is tied to her definition as a woman, particularly in relation to the family, there is an important link between these two types of consciousness.

c. Class consciousness is examined in relation to the first two types of consciousness. Much literature has been devoted to defining and comprehending class consciousness in a broad theoretical framework.[7] For the most part these analyses have focused on the male industrial work force, with the exception of Braverman and Aronowitz.

When examining women office workers, class consciousness takes on quite specific characteristics not usually acknowledged in the literature. While we can use the general outline of Marxist definitions of class consciousness, they must be modified to apply to this particular sector. It is the unique relationship that job and feminist consciousness have to one another that provides the foundation for understanding class consciousness among the female clerical workforce. The existence of a sex-segregated division of labor in the workplace and in the family point to a gender-specific identity for both women and men. Class consciousness of women office workers then must be understood within the context of their experiences within these job and gender categories. Thus, this research contains an examination of how the double role of woman and worker affects the consciousness of respondents and how the three types of consciousness interact and affect one another. If the research finds that the above relationships are strong in working women's organizations, there will be greater insight into the tactics, techniques, and structures that are conducive to organizing women workers who have consistently been considered difficult to organize.

Within the context of these questions an investigation into the following areas provided significant background information necessary to fully understand the development of dissatisfaction and consciousness among the participants in this study:

1. The relationship between changes in the office as a workplace, the increase in women office workers, and their dissatisfaction with their work. An understanding of this relationship necessitates an historical analysis from which the theoretical base of this study is derived. Such an analysis includes a description of the late nineteenth and early twentieth century setting in which industrial expansion under a patriarchal form of capitalism ensured the growth of a clerical work force and the takeover of that sector by women.

2. The rise of a women's office workers' organization. This involves an in-depth description of the following:
   a. History of the organization.
   b. Present structure.
   c. Goals of the organizers.
   d. Tactics to achieve goals.
   e. Strategies to attract participants.
   f. Content of regular meetings, presentations, media exposure, participation in local community activities, etc.

The last 20 years have seen several major influences in women's work world: 1) further expansion of clerical and service industries; 2) introduction of sophisticated electronic machinery (computers and word processors) that have revolutionized the way work is performed, and have profoundly affected the organization of the work place; 3) the renewal of feminism, which has encouraged independence among women in all areas of their lives, including work; and 4) a working women's movement related to but not necessarily the same as the feminist movement or other workers' movements such as unions. The working women's movement is a widespread grassroots effort heavily influenced by the other processes mentioned above, and reflecting growing dissatisfaction among women workers.

Overall, working women's organizations represent attempts to confront the unique experience of workers who experience exploitative conditions both because they are women and because they are working in those sectors of the economy that are highly exploitative. Profound changes are taking place in the labor process at the same time that women are actively seeking changes in their lives. The two processes meet in these new working women's organizations.

RESEARCH METHODS

The primary techniques used in this research were those of participant observation and open-ended interviews.[8] A small scale survey was also conducted. My initial contacts with the organization in this study led to a mutual decision between the group and myself that I not participate directly in the activities of the membership at first, but rather observe the meetings and other activities as unobtrusively as possible. This decision was made in order to protect the operations of the organization from my influence, were I an active participant, and at the same time, allow the members to get used to my presence without expecting any input from me. I was able to maintain a low profile for about four months, but found that as I became a familiar face, more people engaged me in conversation and were curious about my work. I gradually began participating in activities such as helping with mailings and setting up a rally. I found that the greater my active participation, the more open and trusting were the members of the organization.

The observations took place at the monthly general meetings as well as at committee meetings, a steering council session, workshops, mailings, and public events such as National Secretaries' Day, and the Boss Day rally. I also attended the Summer School for Working Women, a nationwide conference sponsored by Working Women. These observations took place over a period of one year. A log was kept of all observations in which as much detail as possible was recorded. I tried to be present at many different types of events that involve this organization so as to get a complete picture of the group, to understand the membership on its own terms, and to limit the chances of selective perception and interpretation.[9] It was agreed that I was to be presented to the membership as a sociologist studying the operations of the organization and the people in it and that the end product of this research would be my Ph.D. dissertation. There was a public assurance of confidentiality and protection of privacy. This introduction took place at the October, 1979 general meeting.

In addition to the observations discussed above, there were three stages of data gathering involving in-depth interviews, a brief survey questionnaire, and further interviews. The first set of interviews was conducted shortly after my introduction to the organization with two of the original founders, two of the paid staff members, and some of the active members. The first interviews supplied me with information necessary to better grasp both the history and the present structure of the group. Through these interviews I was also able to get names of active participants for further interviews. In addition to gaining factual information, I was interested in the respondents' experiences both as women office workers as well as members of the organization. The information gathered in these areas provided data for examining the concepts of dissatisfaction and consciousness. While factual information is relevant here, the body of information I tried to obtain involved the development of attitudes concerning the abovementioned concepts. My decision as to who to interview was based on lists of members of committees and chairs of meetings, by asking my contacts for names of those who are very active and who know a lot about the organization, and by observation of those actively involved at the meetings I attended. In this snowball sampling I found that an interview with one informant led to information about other potential informants and suggestions as to who I should interview next. There was also quota sampling to ensure coverage of various aspects of the organization that might be missed by any particular informant.[10] One informant may have knowledge about a particular committee, but not other aspects of the organization. Other informants may have been absent for a period of time and not be familiar with certain events. Others have special interests such as race or age discrimination. Both minority and older women are actively involved in the organization and I selected what I estimated to be a representative sample of each for interviews. The sampling techniques discussed here served as a protection against significant omissions.

In this first stage standard questions were developed to serve as guides, but I found that keeping the questions open-ended served to allow respondents to emphasize their particular job experiences and attitudes about being working women. This in turn allowed me the freedom to develop categories and theoretical groupings as they emerged from the data. As the interviews proceeded, formal categories of experience and attitudes developed and questions concerning these became more specific. Some questions were added while others were deleted in the final stage of interviewing.

The interviews usually took place on a one-to-one basis before or after general meetings or at other times convenient to the respondents. Arranging interviews proved to be a difficult task, as most women clerical workers have a strictly observed lunch hour and their offices were off-limits for interviews. They had neither the time nor the space, nor was the office an appropriate place to discuss workplace problems. At best, employers would resent the intrusion, and at worst, there was the realistic fear of being fired if it was discovered that the secretary belonged to a working women's organization. Unlike many executives, office workers have neither formal nor informal ways of conducting their own business during the work day. Evenings and weekends often proved inconvenient as well, since precious free time was often spent with families.

I began every interview with a statement assuring the respondents of confidentiality, and have followed through to protect this confidentiality by eliminating names and excluding information that would make it easy to identify the respondent. Interestingly enough, many respondents told me not to worry about confidentiality, explaining that it was about time these issues got aired. All the formal interviews were tape recorded and later transcribed.

Once these interviews were completed and the responses coded, I took two further steps. First I distributed a three-page structured questionnaire to participants attending several different meetings and public events. The purpose of the questionnaire was two-fold: 1) to gather data about the membership that previously did not exist, such as age, race, marital status, income, education; and 2) to get a better idea of the participants' roles in the organization concerning levels of activism, reasons for joining, and the issues they think are important to working women. The questionnaire was not intended to become a source of quantitative data, as I had neither the time nor the money to sample the entire membership. Rather, it was intended to fill in some missing pieces and help me proceed to the next stage of interviewing. With this in mind, I distributed a total of 40 questionnaires to all the participants at a general meeting, several committee meetings, and a public rally. Thirty-four questionnaires were returned. The high rate of return is due in part to the availability of time at a general meeting that enabled people to return them to me the same evening.

This survey provided me with the names of other potential respondents for the next stage of in-depth interviews. Since I had previously interviewed only highly active participants, I selected a comparison group of less active and newly active members in order to assess similarities and differences in their concerns about the workplace, their consciousness about working women's issues, and their expectations of the organization. At the same time, I revised the original interview schedule to increase the focus on attitudes that would give a better idea of their consciousness about their roles as women and workers, an area in which I had been somewhat frustrated in earlier interviews. This last phase of interviews included five people selected from the survey questionnaire who were moderately active or newly active. I also reinterviewed five of the previously interviewed women with the new questions that had been developed since their interviews.

In addition to these interviews, I was able to record small group discussions that took place at a general meeting. Twenty participants were divided into three groups to address such questions as why they joined, what they have learned in the organization, and what they expect of the organization in the future. Much of the discussion involved particular problems women face on the job and ideas about solving those problems. The participants represented a cross section of the membership: staff, officers, rank and file, and new members. I have included these discussions with the other interview data. Data was also made available to me from surveys conducted by the organization itself. Questionnaires distributed throughout the city when the organization was founded, and a more recent survey of bank employees were used as supplements to my own data.

In summary, I interviewed a total of 24 participants or former participants, compiled data from 34 survey questionnaires, incorporated discussions from 20 participants and utilized survey data provided by the organization.

There were several other sources of information that were utilized. There is a growing body of literature, both academic and popular, which describes the world of the female office worker and her attempts at coping with the dissatisfaction found in the workplace.[11] Working women's organizations publish newsletters, reports, and pamphlets, and issue press releases.[12] These sources of information have been utilized as fully as possible, both to round out and to verify the findings of my observations and interviews. I also was able to get access to documents written by the people involved in Baltimore Working Women, including committee reports, membership lists, memos, and correspondence from the national affiliate. By using so many different sources of information, there was less chance for distortion due to selective perception and interpretation, and this enabled a greater saturation of the data.[13]

I have briefly mentioned the issue of confidentiality, but further discussion of this topic is necessary. I initially gained limited access to the group by assuring that I would not try to influence its operations and that I would protect the privacy of both the organization and the individual members. Our initial meeting led to a discussion of the purposes of my research in which I came to realize the political sensitivity of the organization. While the group is both legal and public, it is clear that since it is created to help improve the working conditions of a significant sector of the workforce, there might be opposition to the organization by employers or others who may feel threatened by such an organization. This cannot be seen as an idle concern when one considers similar experiences throughout the history of labor organizing. While I must protect the group from my influence as a participant observer by not becoming too active, I must also ensure that outsiders will not gain greater access to the group than they ordinarily would were I not there. This is an issue concerning both ethics and the credibility of the research. Despite this concern, the organization was generous in allowing the use of their name in this publication.

Further, the interests of the individual members had to be protected from two angles. First, confidentiality must ensure that no one in the group will be able to identify the remarks made by other members so as to protect their standing in the group and their individual privacy. Additionally, these women must be careful not to risk their jobs. Membership in the group in itself is somewhat of a risk; speaking out about their job dissatisfaction and their roles in this organization may increase that risk. Therefore, all precautions possible were taken to protect the privacy of the respondents; no names were used in reporting findings, interviews were held in private, information that could reveal the identity of the respondent was withheld or masked as responsibly as possible.

The methodological techniques described above are particularly useful for studying the processes involved in the growth of dissatisfaction and consciousness. A combination of participant observation, informal interviews and standardized questions show the dynamic interplay between forces that contribute to the experiences and the attitudes of the respondents. These procedures also provide the initial steps necessary if one wishes to design a quantitative study of this particular sector of the labor force.

NOTES

1. Comprehensive discussions of the history of women workers are found in Margery Davies, "Women's Place is at the Typewriter: The Feminization of the Clerical Labor Force," *Radical America* 8 (1974):1–28; Rosalyn Baxandall, Linda Gordon, and Susan Reverby (eds.), *America's Working Women: A Documentary History – 1600 to the Present* (New York: Vintage, 1976); Mary Kathleen Benet, *Secretary: Enquiry into the Female Ghetto* (London: Sedgwick and Jackson, 1972); Nancy Schrom Dye, "Feminism or Unionism? The New York Women's Trade Union League and the Labor Movement," *Feminist Studies* 3 (1975):111–

125; and Alice Kessler-Harris, "Where are the Organized Women Workers?" *Feminist Studies* 3 (1975):92–110.

2. For further discussion, see Gabriel Kolko, "Working Wives: Their Effects on the Structure of the Working Class," *Science and Society* 42 (1978):257–58; and Annemarie Tröger, "The Coalition of Labor Union Women: Strategic Hope, Tactical Despair," in Rosalyn Baxandall, Linda Gordon, and Susan Reverby (eds.), *America's Working Women: A Documentary History — 1600 to the Present* (New York: Vintage, 1976), pp. 390–99.

3. For excellent discussions of women's work and family roles, see Margery Davies and Michael Reich, "On the Relationship Between Sexism and Capitalism" in Richard C. Edwards, Michael Reich, and Thomas E. Weisskopf (eds.), *The Capitalist System: A Radical Analysis of American Society* (Englewood Cliffs, N.J.: Prentice-Hall, 1972), pp. 348–56; Marilyn Power Goldberg "The Economic Exploitation of Women," in Richard C. Edwards, Michael Reich and Thomas E. Weisskopf (eds.) *The Capitalist System: A Radical Analysis of American Society* (Englewood Cliffs, N.J.: Prentice-Hall, 1972), pp. 341–48; Mickey Ellinger and John Rowntree, "More on the Political Economy of Women's Liberation," *Monthly Review* (January 1970), pp. 26–32; Margaret Benston, "The Political Economy of Women's Liberation," *Monthly Review* (September 1969):13–25; and Kolko, "Working Wives."

4. Sally Hillsman Baker, "Women in Blue-Collar and Service Occupations," in Ann H. Stromberg and Shirley Harkess (eds.) *Women Working: Theories and Facts in Perspective* (Palo Alto, California: Mayfield, 1978), pp. 339–76; Davies and Reich, "On the Relationship Between Sexism and Capitalism"; Harry Braverman, *Labor and Monopoly Capital: The Degradation of Work in the Twentieth Century* (New York: Monthly Review Press, 1974); Michel Crozier, *The World of the Office Worker* (Chicago: The University of Chicago Press, 1971); and Benet, *Secretary: Enquiry into the Female Ghetto.*

5. For a thorough discussion of job consciousness, see Sidney M. Peck, "Fifty Years After a Theory of the Labor Movement: Class Conflict in the United States," *The Insurgent Sociologist* 8 (1978):4–13, in reference to Selig Perlman, *A Theory of the Labor Movement.* (New York: Augustus M. Kelley, 1949. Orig. pub. 1928).

6. For further discussion of feminism, see Sheila Rowbotham, *Woman's Consciousness, Man's World* (Middlesex, England: Penguin, 1973); Betty Friedan, *The Feminine Mystique.* (New York: Dell, 1963); Benston, "The Political Economy of Women's Liberation"; Louise Kapp Howe, *Pink Collar Workers: Inside the World of Women's Work* (New York: Avon, 1978); and Jean Tepperman, *Not Servants, Not Machines: Office Workers Speak Out* (Boston: Beacon Press, 1976).

7. Those most useful in this research were Braverman, *Labor and Monopoly Capital*; Wilhelm Reich, "What is Class Consciousness?" in Lee Baxandall (ed.) *Sex-Pol: Essays, 1929–1934* (New York: Vintage Books, 1972), pp. 275–358; Michael Mann, *Consciousness and Action Among the Western Working Class* (London: The Macmillan Press, Ltd., 1980); Gyorgy Lukcas, *History and Class Consciousness*, translated by Rodney Livingstone (Cambridge, Mass.: MIT Press, 1971); and Stanley Aronowitz, *False Promises: The Shaping of America's Working Class Consciousness* (New York: McGraw-Hill, 1973).

8. A comprehensive discussion of participant observation is found in George S. McCall and J. L. Simmons (eds.), *Issues in Participant Observation: A Text and Reader* (Reading, Mass.: Addison-Wesley, 1969).

9. John Lofland, *Analyzing Social Settings: A Guide to Qualitative Observation and Analysis* (Belmont, Calif.: Wadsworth, 1971); Barney G. Glaser and Anselm L. Strauss, *The Discovery of Grounded Theory: Strategies for Qualitative Research* (Chicago: Aldine, 1967); Morris Zelditch, Jr., "Some Methodological Problems of Field Studies," in McCall and Simmons, *Issues in Participant Observation*, pp. 5–19.

10. McCall and Simmons, *Issues in Participant Observation*, pp. 64–65.

11. Aronowitz, *False Promises*; Benet, *Secretary: Enquiry into the Female Ghetto*; Braverman, *Labor and Monopoly Capital*; Crozier, *The World of the Office Worker*; Peter

Drier, "Raises Not Roses: Organizing in the Sexual Ghetto," *In These Times* (June 13-19, 1979):12-13; Evelyn Nakano Glenn and Roslyn L. Feldberg, "Clerical Work: The Female Occupation," in *Women: A Feminist Perspective*, 2nd edition, ed., Jo Freeman (Palo Alto, California: Mayfield, 1979), pp. 313-38; Tepperman, *Not Servants, Not Machines*; Alfred Vogel, "Your Clerical Workers are Ripe for Unionism," in Baxandall, Gordon, and Reverby, *America's Working Women: A Documentary History — 1600 to the Present*, pp. 351-53; The Women's Work Project, *Women Organizing the Office* (New York: A Union for Radical Political Economics Political Education Project, 1978).

12. Sources utilized were Women Employed in Baltimore, *Women Employed: Analysis of the Employment Situation of Women Working in Baltimore Offices* (Baltimore, Maryland: Women Employed in Baltimore, 1978); The Women's Work Project, *Women Organizing the Office*; Working Women, National Association of Office Workers, *Vanished Dreams: Age Discrimination and the Older Woman Worker* (Cleveland, Ohio: Working Women, National Association of Office Workers, 1980).

13. McCall and Simmons, *Issues in Participant Observation*, pp. 77-78.

Chapter 2

Clerical Work in the Late Nineteenth and Twentieth Centuries

WOMEN ENTER THE CLERICAL WORKFORCE

Throughout the early stages of industrial capitalism, prior to the late nineteenth century, those who worked as office clerks were predominantly educated middle-class men. They were separated in status from manual workers, for their occupation afforded them greater prestige. The office setting was one in which the clerk and his employer had a personal and close working relationship, which demanded loyalty and was often rewarded with promotions into management. In other words, the division between clerical work and management was not the tremendous chasm it is today, and the "gentleman" clerk could maintain a middle-class status by virtue of the office being a desirable workplace.[1]

With the growth of monopoly capital in the late nineteenth century, the rise of a large, modern, female-dominated clerical workforce coincided with the expansion of production as a necessary part of the growth of capitalism.[2] This clerical work was separate from the production line, but was tied to it in an interdependent relationship based on an industrial-based capitalist economy. Central to the development of capitalism, the main purpose of which is to create surplus value, is counting and keeping records of profits made by industrial production.

> A portion of the labor of society must therefore be devoted to the accounting of value. As capitalism becomes more complex and develops into its monopoly stage, the accounting of value becomes infinitely more complex. The number of intermediaries between production and consumption increases . . . in some industries the labor expended upon the mere transformation of the form of value (from the commodity form into the form of money or credit) — including the policing, the cashiers,

and collection work, the recordkeeping, the accounting, etc. — begins to approach or surpass the labor used in producing the underlying commodity or service. And finally . . . entire 'industries' come into existence whose activity is concerned with nothing but the transfer of values and the accounting entailed by this.[3]

As business grew, an increasing proportion of the labor force was employed in the paperwork of recordkeeping, correspondence, accounting, and personnel management. The greater demand for clerks, coupled with the increasing number of educated workers prepared to carry out office duties, lowered the prestige of this occupation.[4]

> With the drop in the prestige of clerical work, some of its traditional disadvantages were most keenly felt. Clerks had always been under attack from above and below — scorned by their employers for their pretensions to gentility, they were also despised and resented by working-men because although they too were employees, they pretended to be a cut above the actual laborer. They were the carriers of messages from the boss, his representatives and mouthpieces, although their status did not bring them much of a reward. Indeed, the standards a clerk had to keep up — black coat, white collar, grammar school for his sons — often made him struggle harder to make ends meet than did the worker.[5]

The work that was once performed on an informal basis with much personal contact between clerk and employer, by the end of the nineteenth century was carried out by large numbers of bureaucratically organized and controlled workers who were increasingly female. In fact, the organized management of the office and the feminization of the clerical staff were the two most significant factors influencing the development of the modern office. Moreover, those factors were most effective in further lowering the social status of clerical workers. Office management necessitated the depersonalization of the relationships between worker and employer and the increased specialization and loss of power and general working knowledge of the clerk. Increasingly, office work began to resemble factory work, and the traditional division between mental and manual labor was blurred. Put another way, increased use of office management served to crystalize the distinction between management on the one hand and workers, both mental and manual, on the other.[6]

WHY WOMEN?

At the same time the office was being reorganized, women began to enter the clerical labor force in large numbers. Davies reports that in

1870, 97.15 percent of the clerical workforce were men.[7] By 1890, women made up 21 percent of this occupational group, and by 1920, 50 percent of clerical workers were women.[8] Table 2.1 indicates the growth of women as stenographers and typists, an important segment of the clerical workforce.

The influence of the developments of capitalism in relationship to the historically-based role of patriarchy plays a significant part in women's experience both in and out of the work force. Patriarchy, whose historical origins considerably predate capitalism, played a particularly supportive role once women entered the clerical labor force in large numbers, despite the development of free labor associated with capitalism. In a classic analysis of the relationship of patriarchy and capitalism, Hartmann defines patriarchy as "a set of social relations which has a material base and in which there are hierarchical relations between men, and a solidarity among them, which enable them to control women. Patriarchy is thus the system of male oppression of women."[9] She argues that patriarchy and capitalism create a mutually reinforcing system that benefits both the capitalist and men at the expense of women. Presumably, capitalism engendered an economic system of free labor in which all workers have the same access to jobs and wages, yet throughout capitalist economies we find both occupational and sex segregation and lower wages for women.

Prior to the rise of capitalism, patriarchy enabled men to dominate women through a "direct personal system of control."[10] Under capitalism this control was altered only by changes in the type of organization. Men still dominated. In a fundamental way, capitalism benefits from this arrangement by creating divisions among the workers based on gender. With the ideological approval of the male work force, women have become available as cheap marginal labor.

TABLE 2.1

Stenographers and Typists, for the United States and by Sex: 1870–1930

	Total	Male	Female	Female (percent)
1870	154	147	7	4.5
1880	5,000	3,000	2,000	40.0
1890	33,400	12,100	21,300	63.8
1900	112,600	26,200	86,400	76.7
1910	326,700	53,400	263,300	80.6
1920	615,100	50,400	564,700	91.8
1930	811,200	36,100	775,100	95.6

Source: Margery Davies "Women's Place is at the Typewriter: The Feminization of the Clerical Labor Force," Radical America 8, No. 4 (July–August, 1974) p. 10.

Men, even those in the working class, derive benefits from the continuation of patriarchy under capitalism

> . . . because it enforces lower wages for women in the labor market. Low wages keep women dependent on men because they encourage women to marry. Married women must perform domestic chores for their husbands. Men benefit, then, from both higher wages and the domestic division of labor. This domestic division of labor, in turn, acts to weaken women's position in the labor market.[11]

Thus we find an interdependent relationship between patriarchy and capitalism that manifests itself in the influx of women working in the least rewarding but increasingly important sectors of the economy.

There are several specific reasons why women fulfilled the ever-increasing need for larger office staffs, an area from which they had previously been excluded:

1. The Civil War provided women with the opportunity to replace the male office staff as men went to war.[12]

2. There were a large number of educated women needing work. In fact, more women than men had completed high school at the end of the nineteenth century. "There were literally thousands of women with training that qualified them for jobs that demanded literacy, but who could not find such jobs. Excluded from most professions, these women were readily available for the clerical jobs that started to proliferate at the end of the nineteenth century."[13] Interestingly enough, both middle-class and working-class women entered the clerical workforce. Given the exclusion of middle-class women from professional work and the undesirability of domestic or factory labor among working-class women, both groups of women found employment in offices. As the office became more routinized, the need for highly educated clerks diminished, but by this time, women were dominant as office workers, and other factors became significant in the feminization of clerical work.

3. Probably the most important factor as it pertains to the development of patriarchal capitalism was the consideration that in all areas of employment, women have been cheaper labor than men. It stands to reason that a business interested in making profit would seek the lowest paid labor possible, thus big business was encouraged to hire women to fill clerical positions.[14]

4. The invention of the typewriter both altered the nature of the work process technologically and offered women an opportunity to become identified with a type of work not yet sex-defined. Since neither sex had any experience with this new machinery, women were able to learn its usage with relative ease. Of course the notion that women were more dexterous with their fingers did not hurt this development. Along with the typewriter, the telephone had a tremendous impact in the employment of women in the clerical field.[15]

5. The importance of ideology concerning the acceptability of women work-

ing must also be understood. While there was much ideological encouragement for women to stay in the domestic arena throughout the nineteenth century, by the time large numbers of women entered the work force, and the work itself was losing its prestige through routinization and office management, an accompanying ideology helped ease the transition. Numerous articles at the time attested to the belief that women's "natural passivity makes them ideally suited to the job of carrying out an endless number of routine tasks without a complaint. Furthermore, their docility makes it unlikely that they will aspire to rise very far above their station."[16] This was another way of reassuring male bosses that there was safety in hiring women who would not compete for the boss's job. This was important since there were fewer and fewer opportunities for advancement among office workers. So this ideology was particularly enticing to men wanting to protect their positions in management.[17]

6. Last, the generally accepted patriarchal relationships prevailing in everyday social life and the family were easily carried over into the office. The male boss could legitimately dominate the female clerks, by virtue both of the acceptability of patriarchal relationships in society in general and the similar type of relationship of boss to worker, sexual status aside. In other words, patriarchy as a cultural experience was easily adapted to the office setting, including the notion of having a woman available to fulfill the boss's personal needs.[18]

WOMEN CLERICAL WORKERS TODAY

The trend that began in the late nineteenth century, the expansion of the clerical workforce and the increasing predominance of women in that occupation, continued throughout the twentieth century (see Table 2.2).

Today we find similar conditions prevailing for the woman clerical worker, with even more advanced technology and greater control over the office by management. Big business, being more complex than ever, must rely more heavily upon the paperwork carried out by the office staff, and thus it has become even more important for production to be well organized and managed, and to have the most efficient modern technology available to it. Thus, the work has become more routine and segmented, requiring less skill and working knowledge on the part of the clerk, and ensuring greater control by management. Glenn and Feldberg point out that

> . . . the impetus to subdivide the work process can best be understood not as a response to technological possibilities but as part of a drive to attain control over the cost of clerical services and to assure reliability and standardization in the work process. Since the automated systems require workers to use standard forms, they also make it easier for management to trace errors and assess each worker's productivity, whether it be lines typed or phone calls answered.[19]

TABLE 2.2

The Clerical Labor Force by Sex, 1900–1970 (In thousands of persons 14 years old and over, except as indicated. Census data for 1900, June 1; 1910, April 15; 1920, Jan. 1; 1930–1970, April 1)

	1970		1960		1950	
	16 yrs. old and over	14 yrs. old and over	1970 classi-fication.	1960 classi-fication.	1960 classi-fication.	1950 classi-fication.
Both Sexes	14,208	13,457	9,431	9,617	7,132	7,232
Male	3,748	3,547	3,024	3,120	2,723	2,730
Female	10,461	9,910	6,407	6,497	4,408	4,502
	1940	1930	1920	1910	1900	
Both Sexes	4,982	4,336	3,385	1,987	877	
Male	2,282	2,090	1,771	1,300	665	
Female	2,700	2,246	1,614	688	212	

Source: U.S. Department of Commerce, Bureau of the Census, *Historical Statistics of the United States: Colonial Times to 1970*, Part 1. (Washington, D.C., 1975), pp. 139–40.

Thus we find that while clerical work has expanded in importance to fit the needs of a modern capitalist economy, it has diminished both in terms of the amount of knowledge and power held by the worker as well as by the prestige that accompanies those conditions.[20] In fact, the similarities between clerical work and factory work have grown and become more clear as the working conditions become less desirable and more routinized and controlled by management.[21] Further, it is often pointed out that clerical work has become even lower paid and less secure than manual work, a condition owing partly to the fact that many manual workers are protected by unions, while clerical workers for the most part are not.[22]

ORGANIZED LABOR AND WOMEN WORKERS

The question then arises as to why clerical workers are not part of organized labor, given the objective advantages of higher pay and greater job security. An historical look at the failure to organize clerks and the ideology that discouraged it will provide some insight. The two main conditions suggesting this failure involve, first, the unique position of clerks in relationship to management and production workers and, second, the impact of the increasing proportion of women in clerical positions as the work became less desirable.

Before discussing why these workers did not organize in large numbers, it must be pointed out that they did indeed join unions and form protective organizations. Beginning in the late nineteenth century, postal workers, railway clerks, and retail workers affiliated themselves with various unions such as the AFL and the Knights of Labor.[23]

Office workers united in a variety of organizations around the turn of the century, as did teachers, musicians and actors.[24] Women's labor organizations also arose; the Women's Protective Association and the Women's Trade Union League felt that needs of women workers were not being met by male-dominated unions and set out to meet those needs.[25] The Women's Trade Union League, which was founded in 1903, played an especially important role for women in various types of work at that time. Their goals included unionization for all workers, an eight-hour day, and equal pay for equal work. It was at this time that many women suffered through the long, trying garment workers strikes and several women became prominent as organizers both among the female and male workforce. The separate women's unions and workers' organizations provided women with a solid base for leadership and promotion of the issues of greatest concern to women workers.

By 1920, when 21 percent of the workforce belonged to the unions, 8 percent of all clerical workers were unionized. Broken down by sex, 13 percent of male clericals were unionized, while 3 percent of female clericals were in unions. Overall, 7 percent of all women workers were organized.[26] When union organizing was at full force in the 1930s, many women joined unions, but few ever played significant leadership roles, in part because separate women's unions no longer existed.[27]

Office workers' unions grew stronger during the Depression as part of the CIO but died out during the McCarthy era when they were pressured out of the CIO for having alleged communist affiliations.[28] World War II provided an opportunity for the female workforce to expand, and with it the opportunity to participate in unions.

> During this period . . . a major transformation took place in the structure of work for women accustomed to manual employment. First, largely because of economic necessity, the number and proportion of married women workers rose appreciably, beginning a trend. Secondly, many women workers, married and single, benefited from expanded job opportunities in more skilled and higher-paying industries and were able

to leave lower-quality manual jobs as waitresses, domestics, and sweat-shop workers. Thirdly, black women had an unprecedented opportunity to escape domestic service. Before the war, 72 percent of all employed black women had been household workers; by the war's end, the proportion had dropped to 48 percent, and it has continued to decline.[29]

Nevertheless, equality was limited.

The War Manpower Commission was formally committed to equal pay for equal work, and some union contracts did include equal pay provisions. But the National War Labor Board gave employers a great many loopholes, for example: equal pay did not apply in jobs which were "historically women's work"; it did not apply to inequities in two plants owned by the same company. Wage rates for jobs in which only women worked were "presumed to be correct." The unions generally did not fight this, they did not raise any special demands for women workers, and they didn't set up apprenticeship programs so that women could qualify for jobs after the war. On the contrary, in many instances when a woman joined the union she had to sign an agreement that she would give up her job as soon as the war was over.[30]

These restrictions may help explain why after the war women remained in the labor force, but in lower-paying, more menial jobs than they had held during the war, and did not flock to unions in large numbers.

The last 20 years have seen a slow, steady increase in women joining unions, as Table 2.3 indicates. Furthermore, unions have increased their organizing efforts in white collar occupations overall, and this is reflected in increases in union membership as shown in Table 2.4.

TABLE 2.3

Labor Union Membership by Sex, 1950–1978 (in thousands of persons)

Union Membership	1960	1970	1972	1974	1976	1978
Male	14,733	16,408	16,315	16,985	16,481	16,636
Female	3,340	4,282	4,524	4,600	4,648	5,106
Total	18,117	20,752	20,893	21,643	21,171	21,784
Female (percent)	18.4	20.6	21.7	21.3	22.0	23.4

Source: U.S. Department of Commerce, Bureau of the Census, *Statistical Abstract of the United States, 1980,* 101st Edition. (Washington, D.C.: Government Printing Office, 1980), p. 429.

TABLE 2.4

Percentage White Collar Membership in Unions

1955	1960	1970	1972	1974	1976	1978
13.6	12.2	16.2	16.5	17.4	19.2	18.7

Source: U.S. Department of Commerce, Bureau of the Census, *Statistical Abstract of the United States, 1980,* 101st Edition. (Washington, D.C.: Government Printing Office, 1980), p. 429.

Despite these increases, union membership does not reflect the tremendous growth of women in the clerical sector overall.[31]

As we can see, until recently there has been little organizing activity among women clerical workers, but it is important to remember that white collar workers in general, and female clerical workers specifically, do, in fact have a place in the history of labor organizing, and that the recent growth of interest in organizing is not entirely new and should not be unexpected. Nevertheless, they never organized in as large numbers as blue-collar workers, owing to a number of circumstances that will now be discussed.

Throughout the history of unionizing, clerical workers have always been considered difficult to organize, whether they were men or women. For the most part the reasons for this are tied to the unique position the clerk has in relationship to management, working for but also identifying with the company. Along with that there is a strong identification with the middle class and the status that has traditionally accompanied it. Further, in the period when clerical work was first expanding there were good chances for promotion into management, job security, and a relatively close personal relationship with one's boss. In addition, white-collar workers believed that joining a union was tantamount to lowering one's status by associating with the working class. They believed their mental labor was far more prestigious than the manual work of the blue-collar worker and had little interest in admitting they shared common problems. This attitude was encouraged by management, to whose advantage it was to keep clerical workers out of unions. Several other factors also played a significant role in discouraging unionization. As a group, clerical workers were separated from one another by work roles, status hierarchies within the office, and the organization of the office in general, thus making it harder to unionize. In addition, as is true with all organizing efforts, the realistic fear of reprisal from the employer and the potential disruption of relationships with co-workers made it risky for the worker to join a union.[32]

As more women entered the clerical workforce, the potential for unionization weakened even further. There was a strong ideological position supported not only by employers but by male unionists and the women clerks themselves against organizing women. The generally accepted notion of women's inferiority supported the belief that since women did not deserve as much as men, they should not get as much — in this case, money or good jobs.[33] The strong identification of women with the home and family life made it difficult for a woman (or anyone else) to see a job as more than a temporary activity before marriage or between births of children.[34] Also, being socialized into passivity and obedience to authority, women were not inclined to take overly strong assertive roles.[35]

Despite the increase of women working for wages, it is clear that the prevailing ideology still did not see them as workers, but first and foremost as women with traditional responsibilities and behavior. This ideology has been supported by the paternalistic relationship between employer and female worker and encouraged by the patriarchal context in which capitalism operates. Paternalism had been an important part of the accepted working relationship between clerk and boss in the small office of the nineteenth century. It was easily carried over to the more modern office as women increased in number and traditional sex roles were maintained. In these offices we often find that

> . . . managers make demands at their own discretion and arbitrarily recruit secretaries on the basis of appearance, personality, and other subjective factors rather than on skill, expect personal service, exact loyalty, and make secretaries part of their private retinue . . . There may be no job descriptions, as there are for managerial positions, that help match the person's skills to the job or insure some uniformity of demands across jobs, so that there are often no safeguards to exploitation, no standards for promotion other than personal relationships, and no way of determining if a secretary can be moved to another job (all barriers to mobility out of the secretarial ranks for women).[36]

Beyond ideology, several other factors discouraged the unionization of women workers. Protective labor laws made it appear that women did not need the protection of unions.[37] Even more importantly, male-controlled unions themselves had mixed feelings about women.

> Since employers clearly had important economic incentives for hiring women, male trade unions felt they had either to eliminate that incentive, or to offer noneconomic reasons for restricting women's labor-force participation. In the early 1900s they tried to do both. In order to reduce the economic threat, organized labor repeatedly affirmed a commitment to unionize women wage earners and to extract equal pay for

them. Yet trade unionists simultaneously argued that women's contributions to the home and their duties as mothers were so valuable that women ought not to be in the labor force at all. Their use of the home-and-motherhood argument had two negative effects: it sustained the self-image on which the particular exploitation of women rested, and it provided employers with a weapon to turn against the working class as a whole.[38]

Thus, the real economic threat to men of women entering the workforce at lower wages was reduced by an appeal to the ideology concerning traditional female roles.

There have also been practical considerations that have made it difficult for unions to organize clerical workers. In the past much of the organizing in offices took place in close proximity to organized blue-collar workplaces, providing office workers with direct contact with successful unionization experiences. More recently the office and factory have become physically separated, while becoming structurally more alike, making it difficult to provide close encounters with unions already established. Furthermore, the office itself has become divided and the workers separated hierarchically, making unified efforts difficult.[39]

The unions have been slow to recognize or address issues of most concern to women office workers as they continue to use traditional organizing tactics. In their organizing efforts unions have emphasized ". . . . pay, hours, fringe benefits, and working conditions."[40] On the other hand, surveys have shown rather different concerns of women clerical workers: "respect shown to employees, absence of favoritism, the kind of work they do, the 'atmosphere' at the company . . . the amount of work expected of them."[41] In addition, working women's organizations have found their membership to be concerned with such issues as respect, job descriptions, equal pay for equal work, maternity benefits, promotions, on-the-job training and sex discrimination.[42] Few of the unions have women in leadership positions, making it even more difficult for women to identify with union efforts. At the same time, management has often responded with a variety of tactics such as raising salaries, increasing fringe benefits, or getting rid of militants when they are feeling the threat of organizing campaigns.[43]

THE NEW WOMEN OFFICE WORKERS' MOVEMENT: WHY NOW?

As we enter the 1980s, the traditional sex-based division of labor prevails, with women dominating the low-paid clerical and service occupations. The impact of the combination of the growth of large industries with increasing control by management and an advanced technology that affects the organization and procedures of the work itself is most keenly felt by the women who carry out the paperwork.

There are several factors that have contributed to the present rise of working women's organizations. An understanding of the material conditions faced by a woman on the job, in her family and in society in general coupled with a look at ideology and opportunities for activism will help explain the rise of such a movement. These issues will be examined briefly here, and elaborated on in a discussion of the findings of this research.

In the clerical field, women make up between 75 percent to nearly 100 percent of the workers in most occupations. Data on these occupational categories from 1976 show the following percentages of women in female-dominated clerical jobs: bank tellers, 91.1 percent; bookkeepers, 90 percent; cashiers, 87.17 percent; office machine operators, 73.7 percent; secretaries-typists, 98.5 percent.[44] Women clericals receive 64.1 percent of the salaries earned by men in the same occupations.[45] While women clerical workers do not earn less then women in most other occupations, they do earn less than men, not only in the clerical field, but in every field except farming.[46] In those occupations in which men predominate, the gap in wages is even greater than that of clericals (see Table 2.5).

Furthermore, over the years there has been a relative decline in pay for clerical workers as compared to blue-collar workers. Whereas white-collar workers once relied upon their higher salaries as one indicator of higher status and relative job satisfaction, today their salaries are often lower than those in the manual trades. There are several reasons for this:

TABLE 2.5

Wages for Female Clerical Workers Compared to Wages for
Men in Male-Dominated Occupations

	Percent males in occupation	Weekly earnings wages for males (in dollars)	Percent income compared to female clerical workers
Professional/ technology	58.0	299	49.9
Managerial- Administrative	79.2	320	45.9
Sales	57.1	244	60.2
Craft	95.2	243	60.5

Source: U.S. Department of Labor, Bureau of Labor Statistics, U.S. Working Women: A Databook. (Washington, D.C.: Government Printing Office Bulletin, 1977), p. 34.

As women entered the clerical workforce as cheap sources of labor, the companies justified paying them less than men because of their sex status. This was especially helpful to management, given the tremendous increase in the need for clerical workers as the economy expanded. This historical precedent has remained essentially unchanged. The lack of unionization among clerical workers also helps explain the lower salaries. Belonging to a union is of greater significance in terms of pay for women than for men. As of 1970, overall, women union members earned salaries 70 percent higher than nonunion women, while for men, union membership meant a 30 percent improvement in salary. In white-collar work specifically, women union members received 44 percent more in wages than nonunion women, and for men the figure was 8 percent.[47] The growing awareness among working women of these salary differences[48] as well as increased consumption needs and the greater dependence upon the income of working women, whether married or single, has also contributed to dissatisfaction with wages among clerical workers.

It is well documented that women tend to enter the labor force during periods of economic crisis as more sources of income are needed to maintain their families.[49]

> The key to the economic position of the now preponderant working wives is not merely their own mediocre income but that of their husbands as well. That women enter the labor market especially in periods of economic adversity confirms the fact that working class families are responding to deepening economic difficulties that men cannot resolve singly or collectively. The manifold consequences of this adjustment process are crucial to an understanding of the post-[World War II]war economic experience. This process has compelled the women of the working class to play the role of a surplus labor army, providing ample cheap labor for new or expanded kinds of work that can only be regarded as satellite functions of a classic proletariat.[50]

Women themselves are aware of the economic necessity of working for wages. The Monthly Labor Review in 1976 reports that 42 percent of working wives do so, according to their own assessment, for "financial necessity" and another 17 percent work to "earn extra money."[51] In fact, the most significant increase in women workers since the end of World War II is among married women, and most recently among women with young children.[52] This indicates the increased necessity for more than one adult to bring in wages (see Table 2.6).

While women go to work to provide for their families' needs during economic crises and periods of high unemployment, at the same time their employment leads to greater consumption by providing a greater number of people with more spending money.[53] Nevertheless, women are finding

TABLE 2.6

Married Women (Husband Present) in the Labor Force, by Presence and Age of Children: 1960–1979

Presence and Age of Children	Number (millions)					
	1960	1965	1970	1975	1978	1979
Women, husband present	12.3	14.7	18.4	21.1	22.8	23.8
With no children under 18 yr.	5.7	6.8	8.2	9.7	10.3	11.0
With children 6–17 yr. only	4.1	4.8	6.3	7.0	7.8	8.1
With children under 6 yr.	2.5	3.1	3.9	4.4	4.6	4.8
Also with children 6–17 yr.	1.4	1.7	2.0	1.9	2.0	2.1

Presence and Age of Children	Labor Force Participation Rate*					
	1960	1965	1970	1975	1978	1979
Women, husband present	30.5	34.7	40.8	44.4	47.6	49.4
With no children under 18 yr.	34.7	38.3	42.2	43.9	44.7	46.7
With children 6–17 yr. only	39.0	42.7	49.2	52.3	57.2	59.1
With children under 6 yr.	18.6	23.3	30.3	36.6	41.6	43.2
Also with children 6–17 yr.	18.9	22.8	30.5	34.2	40.9	41.6

*Married women in the labor force as percent of married women in the population.

Note: As of March. Beginning 1975, data not comparable with earlier years due to the use of 1970 census data in estimation procedure. Based on Current Population Survey conducted by the Bureau of the Census.

Source: U.S. Department of Commerce, Bureau of the Census, Statistical Abstract of the United States, 1980, p. 403.

their wages and job opportunities inadequate to their needs. As they work outside the home their need for clothing, transportation, childcare, and more efficient machinery to perform household chores increases.

One way office workers have traditionally increased their wages has been through promotion into management.[54] The potential for promotions has decreased significantly due to the structural organization of the modern office coupled with new technology that serves to divide management from routine workers more than ever.[55] There are simply fewer management jobs available compared to the number of clericals and those that exist are often filled by recruiting men from outside the company. Furthermore, today's clerical worker finds herself in an isolated, impersonal setting often physically separated from supervisors. Consequently, getting promoted on the basis of one's individual qualities has become rare. The physical separation has also contributed to the "dead-end" nature of clerical jobs, with no training available for clericals to learn new skills.[56]

The historical basis of this important division between management and clerical workers lies in the belief that it is considered

> . . . "wasteful," from the capitalist point of view, to have a manager spend time typing letters, opening mail, sending parcels, making travel arrangements, answering the telephone, etc., when these duties could be performed by labor power hired at anywhere from one-third to one-fiftieth of the remuneration of the manager . . . [57]

Using the same reasoning, we find clerical staffs subdivided by specialized tasks. This is an additional advantage to management, allowing greater control over the office staff due to the ability to limit the workers' contact with one another. New technologies, particularly computers, have helped solidify this division. Highly computerized offices generally have a few programmers and technicians, usually male, and a large staff of women carrying out the boring repetitive work required to retrieve data. The sharp divisions between these two groups is based on skill, sex, and often, race.

The advantage to management of advanced technology and a highly stratified division of labor in the office lies in increased speed and efficiency in the work process and greater control over the clerical staff. Speed and efficiency for management translates into deskilling of the work itself, and loss of job security for the clerk. There are several possible effects of deskilling on the relative dissatisfaction of the worker with her job. Tepperman suggests that the less skill needed the more willing the worker will be to accept otherwise unsatisfactory working conditions.[58] On the other hand, deskilling may lead to discontent as the work becomes more boring and the worker more isolated. As for greater control over the clerical staff, technology and the subdivided structure of the office operate together to lessen the decision-making power of the office worker and increase profits through the ability to measure the amount and speed of work.[59]

The combination of low pay, minimal chances for promotion, deskilling of work, and greater control over the workplace by management have provided concrete incentives for clerical workers to organize around these issues. But there are other incentives as well, that have a significant effect on the consciousness of women workers even on those who are not necessarily experienced on the job. The serious challenge to the traditional role of women in the family, the rise of the women's movement, and the accompanying changes in ideology, will be discussed in terms of their contribution to the rise of the women office workers' movement.

It is impossible to separate an analysis of women's increased participation in the clerical sector of the labor force from their family roles. Women are having fewer children and living longer than ever before in history. Much work previously carried out as household tasks has been made easier through advanced technology or removed entirely from the domestic arena into the public service sector. Therefore, women have more time during their lifespans to participate in wage work.[60] Nevertheless, an ideology supporting traditional women's roles in the home, perpetrated by sex-role socialization has channeled both the direction of the work women do as well at the attitudes that are held about their work. Essentially, women have been taught to be submissive both at home and at work. A strong orientation towards successful marriage as a woman's primary goal forces their career goals into a secondary position. This inevitably affects a woman's choice of occupation and helps explain her willingness to work for low wages.

> As they feel responsible to continue their role as housewives and mothers while working (and there are no facilities to relieve them of this burden), they are forced to accept a very low economic position and, even if skilled, to be exploited as a cheap labor force. They are bound to search for work near their homes and very often for only part of the day or the year. Thus they are in a poor bargaining position vis-a-vis their employers. This situation is further exacerbated by the tendency of many women to work until their children are born, drop out of the work force for ten, fifteen, even twenty years, and then return to work after their children are grown. Thus they never acquire seniority or qualify for retirement and other benefits — employers, who are reluctant to promote women to prestigious or high paying jobs, have an excuse not to do so.[61]

The combination of limited availability of and preparation for jobs and the restrictions experienced by women based on their submissive sex-role identity places them comfortably into clerical work. In fact, the very behavior that reinforces traditional sex roles in the home becomes suitable behavior for the office, both in terms of the patriarchal nature of the power structure found there and in terms of the types of tasks expected of women who fill the roles of housewives and clerical workers.

> Filing is like washing dishes and induces the same sense of frustration. Typing a perfect letter is as transient an achievement as cooking an egg. These things are done with little conscious attention; the routine becomes automatic, and the mind wanders into its own escapist paths, which are different for the secretary and the housewife only because of their different ages and circumstances . . . Both kinds of work take place when the master is away; most of his presence is spent giving orders for the next round of work. The tasks are performed on his behalf but do not depend on him personally . . .[62]

Given the mutually reinforcing nature of women's work in the home and the office, it is not surprising that just as some housewives have been expressing dissatisfaction with their lives publicly since the early 1960s, clerical workers too are less than happy at their jobs. Furthermore, there is an additional burden placed on the working mother. Her

> . . . culturally defined role is a non-market one, the practical day-to-day care of children. While men can comfort themselves with the thought that "at least I'm providing for my family," working women fear that "I'm neglecting the children, too." As a result, women experience all the alienation faced by any worker under capitalism, face a conflict rather than a reinforcement of cultural values, and are not even financially rewarded for their discomfort.[63]

The frustration and conflict women feel as they try to combine traditional family life with the necessity of working for a wage in an insecure, low-paying job is exacerbated by the increased dependence on women's incomes as more families break up and women become heads of households, often being the sole support of their children. Even families that stay together, particularly working-class families, must face greater economic hardships as inflation and unemployment skyrocket. We therefore find paradoxical expectations. On the one hand, traditional sex roles make it easy for women to accept the clerical work role, but leaving the home to go to work creates its own set of expectations and problems and raises issues that leave the woman questioning those traditional roles, feeling both the potential for achievement and the frustration of being locked into work roles that do not permit that potential to develop.

The rise of the working women's movement cannot be explained only by economic circumstances, material conditions of the office, and dissatisfaction with traditional sex roles. There must also be a collective awareness of these dissatisfactions. In this, the women's movement has played a decisive role in several respects. In the early years the movement consisted primarily of students, young professional women and some middle-class housewives. Its emphasis on small group consciousness raising, interpersonal relationships, and "making it" in a man's world did not speak to the most important issues facing women clerical workers or working-class women in general. The distortion of women's issues by the male-dominated mass media did not help endear the movement to working-class women who often found it threatening. Given the circumstances, it is not surprising that many working women expressed hostility toward the movement.[64] At first, office workers were often isolated from feminists or had limited and negative experiences.

> The only contact with such women may well have been in the office, where they were either scorned and patronized by a woman who had made it, or annoyed by the attempts of a 'radical' girl to enlist supporters

for the cause. Neither one was likely to show much understanding or
sympathy for the real issues in the secretary's life . . .[65]

As a result, working-class women have developed rather mixed feelings
about the women's movement. One study of these attitudes reports that
while many working-class women support a woman's right to work outside the home and would not choose homemaking as their vocation if they
were to start over again, they nevertheless feel that the women's movement "belittles the homemaker." Further, they often support the goals of
the movement but not the tactics used to achieve these goals.[66]

In recent years the feminist movement has redirected much of its attention toward those women it had previously ignored, hoping to unify
women from different classes and ethnic groups. The maturation of the
movement led to new goals calling for the collective improvement of all
women, and began to pay particular attention to those groups of women
it had been accused of ignoring. In doing so, feminists discovered that
clerical workers were even more devalued than women in professional
work and subject to even greater control through more restrictive work
roles which typified the worst of stereotyped assumptions about women.[67]

In general it can be said that the women's movement has affected
clerical workers in both direct and indirect ways. Clearly, it has had a
pervasive influence on the consciousness of many working women, despite
some of the negative effects previously mentioned. Seeing women act
assertively on their own behalf in a variety of situations has encouraged
many other women to redefine their goals and interests. "Employers who
thought their 'girls' were immune to the subversive ideas of 'feminism'
find those women suddenly making demands — to be treated with respect,
to earn more money, to define their duties, to advance, and to get fringe
benefits that other workers enjoy."[68]

On a more concrete level, there has often been much direct mutual
support between feminist groups such as the National Organization for
Women and working women's organizations. Many unions have women's
caucuses, groups such as the Coalition of Labor Union Women, which cut
across the spectrum of union membership. The awareness of the necessity
of this sort of unifying effort has so far managed to override potential conflicts due to differences in life style or positions or some feminist issues
such as abortion.[69]

CONCLUSION

In this chapter I have presented a brief sketch of the role women have
played in the office historically and at present, in order to set the stage for
understanding the rise of the working women's movement. As we have

seen, a combination of factors have led to this development. It has been observed that the expansion of the office under modern capitalism necessitated hiring cheap labor to do the paperwork required for maintaining large-scale industrial enterprises as well as new forms of production, such as the service sector.

As the office grew in size and complexity, new forms of management and control limited the responsibilities, skills, and potential for promotion into management for clerical workers. This expansion has continued throughout the twentieth century, as has the increased employment of women to the clerical sector. In trying to understand what objective conditions gave rise to the current office workers' movement, it was noted that there was limited but somewhat effective organizing among clericals earlier in this century. Nevertheless, it was short lived and lacked support from unions, for the most part.

Today, we find a number of conditions that help explain the current growth of the office-workers' movement. Presently, more women work out of economic necessity than ever before. Thus, there is growing concern about adequate pay, job security, promotions, and overall working conditions. As more women enter the labor force, the workplace has become more problematic for them. The changes in office structure, particularly the bureaucratization of control and the entry of new technologies, has led to greater dissatisfaction among clericals. Moreover, women workers must balance family life and work life in new ways, both in terms of practical daily living as well as in conforming to a traditional ideology that may expect them to play roles contradictory to their material needs. With the help of a vocal women's movement, many women have begun to focus on those issues that most directly affect their experiences, and to find other women who share those experiences and hope to improve the conditions in which working women find themselves.

The organizations that have grown out of these combined factors have actively moved to improve working conditions for women office workers. Their rapid growth is testimony to the recognition among clericals that such groups can help them. The remaining chapters are devoted to an in-depth look at the operation of one such organization, and the experiences and ideas of its membership. With this focus we will gain a better understanding of the dissatisfactions experienced by office workers, the actions they take to decrease dissatisfaction, and their consciousness of their roles as women workers in the context of society as a whole.

NOTES

1. For a comprehensive examination of the experiences and consciousness of clerical workers in the nineteenth century, see David Lockwood, *The Blackcoated Worker: A Study In Class Consciousness* (London: Ruskin House, George Allen and Unwin, Ltd., 1958).

2. Harry Braverman, *Labor Monopoly Capital: The Degradation of Work in the Twentieth Century* (New York: Monthly Review Press, 1974), pp. 293–302.

3. Ibid., p. 302.

4. Mary Kathleen Benet, *Secretary: Enquiry into the Female Ghetto* (London: Sedgwick and Jackson, 1972) pp. 40–41.

5. Ibid., p. 38.

6. Braverman, *Labor and Monopoly Capital*, pp. 315–26.

7. Margery Davies, "Womens Place is at the Typewriter: The Feminization of the Clerical Labor Force," *Radical America* 8 (1974):2.

8. Ibid., p. 7.

9. Heidi Hartmann, "Capitalism and Patriarchy, and Job Segregation by Sex," *Signs: Journal of Women in Culture and Society*, vol. 1, no. 3, part 2 (Spring 1976):138.

10. Ibid.

11. Hartmann, "Capitalism and Patriarchy," p. 139.

12. Davies, "Women's Place is at the Typewriter," p. 7; Evelyn Nakano Glenn and Roslyn L. Feldberg, "Clerical Work: The Female Occupation," in *Women: A Feminist Perspective*, 2nd edition, ed. Jo Freeman (Palo Alto, California: Mayfield, 1979), p. 317.

13. Davies, "Women's Place is at the Typewriter," p. 2.

14. Ibid., p. 20; Glenn and Feldberg, "Clerical Work: The Female Occupation," p. 322.

15. Benet, *Secretary: Enquiry into the Female Ghetto*, p. 39; Davies, "Women's Place is at the Typewriter," p. 7.

16. Davies, "Women's Place is at the Typewriter," pp. 18–19.

17. Glenn and Feldberg, "Clerical Work: The Female Occupation," p. 320; Jean Tepperman, *Not Servants, Not Machines: Office Workers Speak Out* (Boston: Beacon Press, 1976), pp. 50–51; Davies, "Women's Place is at the Typewriter," pp. 18–19.

18. Tepperman, *Not Servants, Not Machines*, pp. 50–51; Davies, "Women's Place is at the Typewriter," pp. 13–19.

19. Glenn and Feldberg, "Clerical Work: The Female Occupation," p. 324.

20. Virginia L. Olesen and Frances Katsuranis, "Urban Nomads: Women in Temporary Clerical Services," in *Women Working: Theories and Facts in Perspective*, ed. Ann H. Stromberg and Shirley Harkess (Palo Alto, California: Mayfield, 1978), pp. 316–38.

21. Stanley Aronowitz, *False Promises: The Shaping of America's Working Class Consciousness* (New York: McGraw-Hill, 1973), pp. 301–02; Glenn and Feldberg, "Clerical Work: The Female Occupation," p. 324; Braverman, *Labor and Monopoly Capital*, pp. 305–10.

22. Aronowitz, *False Promises*, pp. 297–99.

23. Everett M. Kassalow, "White-Collar Unionism in the United States," in *White-Collar Trade Unions. Contemporary Developments in Industrialized Societies*, ed. Adolf Sturmthal (Chicago: University of Illinois Press, 1967), pp. 318–29.

24. Ibid., pp. 318–29.

25. Patricia Cayo Sexton, "Workers (Female) Arise! On Founding the Coalition of Labor Union Women," *Dissent* 21 (1974):386–87; Joyce Maupin, *Working Women and Their Organizations: 150 Years of Struggle* (Berkeley, Cal.: Union Wage Educational Committee, 1974), p. 8.

26. Ruth Milkman, "Organizing the Sexual Division of Labor: Historical Perspectives on 'Women's Work' and the American Labor Movement," *Socialist Review*, no. 49 (April, 1980), pp. 121–22.

27. Maupin, *Working Women and Their Organizations*, p. 12.

28. Kassalow, "White-Collar Unionism in the United States," p. 329; Tepperman, *Not Servants, Not Machines*, pp. 164–69.

29. Sally Hillsman Baker, "Women in Blue-Collar and Service Occupations," in Ann H.

Stromberg and Shirley Harkess (eds.) *Women Working: Theories and Facts in Perspective* (Palo Alto, California: Mayfield, 1978), pp. 340–41.

30. Maupin, *Working Women and Their Organizations*, p. 15.

31. U.S. Department of Labor, Bureau of Labor Statistics. *U.S. Working Women: A Databook* (Washington, D.C., Government Printing Office Bulletin, 1977), p. 9.

32. Major points concerning lack of unionization among clerical workers are drawn from Albert A. Blum, Martin Estey, James W. Kuhn, Wesley A. Wildman, and Leo Troy, *White-Collar Workers* (New York: Random House, 1971); Benet, *Secretary: Enquiry Into the Female Ghetto*; Lockwood, *The Blackcoated Worker*; Tepperman, *Not Servants, Not Machines*; Michel Crozier, *The World of the Office Worker* (Chicago: The University of Chicago Press, 1971); Rosabeth Moss Kanter, "Women and the Structure of Organizations: Explorations in Theory and Behavior," in Marcia Millman and Rosabeth Moss Kanter (eds.) *Another Voice: Feminist Perspectives on Social Life and Social Sciences*. (New York: Anchor Books, 1975), pp. 34–74; Phyllis Marynick Palmer and Sharon Lee Grant, *The Status of Clerical Workers: A Summary Analysis of Research Findings and Trends*. (Washington, D.C.: Women's Studies Program, George Washington University and Business and Professional Women's Foundation, 1979); David Wagner. "Clerical Workers: How 'Unorganizable' Are They?" *Labor Center Review*, vol. 2, no. 1 (Spring/Summer 1979):20–50.

33. Tepperman, *Not Servants, Not Machines*, p. 66.

34. Ibid.; Alice Kessler-Harris, "Where are the Organized Women Workers?" *Feminist Studies* 3 (1975):94.

35. Ibid., p. 94; Tepperman, *Not Servants, Not Machines*, p. 66. For further discussion, see Palmer and Grant, *The Status of Clerical Workers*; Benet, *Secretary: Enquiry Into the Female Ghetto*.

36. Kanter, "Women and the Structure of Organizations," pp. 41–42.

37. Kessler-Harris, "Where Are the Organized Women Workers?" p. 105.

38. Ibid., p. 95.

39. Wagner, "Clerical Workers: How 'Unorganizable' Are They?" p. 36.

40. Ibid.

41. Blum et al., *White-Collar Workers*, p. 41.

42. Working Women, *The Bill of Rights for Women Office Workers* (Cleveland, Ohio: Working Women, A National Association of Office Workers).

43. Wagner, "Clerical Workers: How 'Unorganizable' Are They?" pp. 42–43; Tepperman, *Not Servants, Not Machines*, pp. 133–38.

44. U.S. Department of Labor, *U.S. Working Women*, p. 9.

45. Ibid., p. 34.

46. See also Palmer and Grant, *The Status of Clerical Workers*.

47. Edna E. Raphael, "Working Women and Their Membership in Labor Unions," *Monthly Labor Review* 97 (1974):27; Olesen and Katsuranis, "Urban Nomads," p. 319.

48. See Women Employed in Baltimore, *Women Employed: Analysis of the Employment Situation of Women Working in Baltimore Offices* (Baltimore, Maryland: Women Employed in Baltimore, 1978); Elinor Langer, "The Women of the Telephone Company," *New York Review of Books* 14, nos. 5 and 6 (Boston, Mass.: The New England Free Press, reprinted pamphlet, 1970), p. 20.

49. Gabriel Kolko, "Working Wives: Their Effects on the Structure of the Working Class," *Science and Society* 42 (1978):262–68; Baker, "Women in Blue-Collar and Service Occupations," p. 20.

50. Kolko, "Working Wives," p. 271.

51. Ibid., p. 263.

52. Kolko, "Working Wives," p. 266.

53. Benet, *Secretary: Enquiry into the Female Ghetto*, p. 150; Kolko, "Working Wives," p. 273.

54. Langer, "The Women of the Telephone Company," p. 20; Tepperman, *Not Servants, Not Machines*, pp. 42–43.

55. Blum et al., *White-Collar Workers*, p. 17; Kassalow, "White-Collar Unionism in the United States," pp. 356–58; Tepperman, *Not Servants, Not Machines*, pp. 41–42; Glenn and Feldberg, "Clerical Work: The Female Occupation," p. 315.

56. Tepperman, *Not Servants, Not Machines*, pp. 42–43.

57. Braverman, *Labor and Monopoly Capital*, p. 342.

58. Tepperman, *Not Servants, Not Machines*, p. 59.

59. For further discussion on the relationship between specialization, technology, and control in the office, see Braverman, *Labor and Monopoly Capital*; Tepperman, *Not Servants, Not Machines*; Glenn and Feldberg, "Clerical Work: The Female Occupation"; Benet, *Secretary: Enquiry into the Female Ghetto*; Kassalow, "White-Collar Unionism"; Blum et al., "White-Collar Workers" Alfred Vogel, "Your Clerical Workers Are Ripe for Unionism," in Rosalyn Baxandall, Linda Gordon, and Susan Reverby (eds.) *America's Working Women: A Documentary History – 1600 to the Present* (New York: Vintage, 1976).

60. Kolko, "Working Wives," pp. 261–62.

61. Marilyn Power Goldberg, "The Economic Exploitation of Women," in Richard C. Edwards, Michael Reich, and Thomas E. Weisskopf (eds.) *The Capitalist System: A Radical Analysis of American Society* (Englewood Cliffs, N.J.: Prentice-Hall, 1972), p. 343.

62. Benet, *Secretary: Enquiry into the Female Ghetto*, pp. 74–75. The relationship between sex-role socialization and occupational experience for women is discussed in Margery Davies and Michael Reich, "On the Relationship between Sexism and Capitalism," in Richard C. Edwards, Michael Reich, and Thomas Weisskopf (eds.) *The Capitalist System: A Radical Analysis of American Society* (Englewood Cliffs, N.J.: Prentice-Hall, 1972); Kanter, "Women and the Structure of Organizations"; Olesen and Katsuranis, "Urban Nomads"; Goldberg, "The Economic Exploitation of Women"; Benet, *Secretary: Enquiry into the Female Ghetto*.

63. Mickey Ellinger and John Rowntree, "More on the Political Economy of Women's Liberation," *Monthly Review* (January 1970) from reprinted pamphlet, *The Political Economy of Women's Liberation* (San Francisco: United Front Press), p. 18.

64. Sexton, "Workers (Female) Arise!" p. 382.

65. Benet, *Secretary: Enquiry into the Female Ghetto*, p. 120.

66. Sexton, "Workers (Female) Arise!" p. 383.

67. Tepperman, *Not Servants, Not Machines*, pp. 169–74.

68. Ibid., p. 68.

69. Key points made about the women's movement and clerical workers were obtained from Annmarie Tröger, "The Coalition of Labor Union Women: Strategic Hope, Tactical Despair," in Rosalyn Baxandall, Linda Gordon, and Susan Reverby (eds.) *America's Working Women: A Documentary History – 1600 to the Present* (New York: Vintage, 1976); Raphael, "Working Women and Their Membership in Labor Unions"; Peter Drier, "Raises Not Roses: Organizing in the Sexual Ghetto," *In These Times* (June 13–19, 1979), pp. 12–13. Benet, *Secretary: Enquiry into the Female Ghetto*; Tepperman, *Not Servants, Not Machines*; Pamela Roby, "Sociology and Women in Working-Class Jobs," in *Another Voice: Feminist Perspectives on Social Life and Social Science*, ed. Marcia Millman and Rosabeth Moss Kanter. (New York: Anchor Books, 1975); Sexton, "Workers (Female) Arise!"

Chapter 3

The Working Women's Movement Today

THE NATIONAL ORGANIZATION

The most recent development of women's office workers' organizations came about in the 1970s, the first being "9 to 5" in Boston in 1973. Since then, in large and small cities, groups have organized to examine and act on issues concerning women office workers. A major impetus to organize arose when it appeared that affirmative action programs were being watered down by the Ford administration. During the mid-1970s various groups began to work together and with public interest groups to form the National Women's Employment Project. The main issue addressed in this project were EEO regulations and banking employment. The group agreed that there was a need for expansion of working women's organizations and proceeded on a project to assess the viability of such action. From 1976 to 1977 various organizing techniques were tried out in cities in New England and out of this emerged the national organization, Working Women, National Association of Office Workers, sponsored by groups in San Francisco, Boston, and Cleveland. While some groups dropped away in this process, several new groups were created.

The national organization carried out successful organizing campaigns in what they designated as strategically targeted cities such as Pittsburgh, Los Angeles, Seattle, and Baltimore. At the same time, other groups arose spontaneously. By 1980, there were 12 organizations affiliated nationally with a membership of 8,000 individuals.

At the time this research was conducted the national group's emphasis in terms of issues involved older working women, the banking industry, and EEO regulations. On a concrete level the national organization provides support for local groups, primarily in the form of training organizers and leaders and raising funds. A conference is held every summer where workshop training is provided. Other national events such as National Secretaries' Day and the 1979 nationwide tour with Jane Fonda help local groups promote unified campaigns and provide information and materials to use in local organizing.

Information provided by both the national organization and local groups indicates great similarity of interest from city to city. Most groups have had campaigns organized around the banking industry, the primary issues being pay, job postings, and promotions. Another area that has received much attention is the insurance field. Both banking and insurance hire women in most of the low-level positions, and, of course, the work in these industries is for the most part clerical. Several local organizations have had success in winning back pay and job postings in a variety of workplaces by working with state and federal government agencies and using pressure tactics.

The national organization and many of the local organizations provide printed information, newsletters, pamphlets on specific work conditions, and surveys of the workforce in their respective cities to their membership and other interested parties.

Most of the local groups have a brochure whose purpose is to attract new members. A sample of these brochures shows much consistency in their content. Generally, there is a description of the economic and working conditions of women either nationally, locally or both, which contains statistics on pay and occupational sex segregation. The appeal to join is accompanied by specific goals of the organization and means to employ these goals. The goals are phrased in general terms such as ". . . to win fair, equal and dignified treatment on the job. . . ." This may be further explained in terms of increasing wages, promotions and respect, and in acquiring job descriptions and job postings. In fact, in all the literature these particular issues are raised most frequently.

Next, there is a description of how these goals are to be achieved, which falls into two categories. One approach is on a large public scale in which the workplace is investigated and/or pressured on issues related to their female employees and in which government agencies, whose purpose it is to enforce related laws, are monitored and pressured to enforce these laws. The other approach is directed toward individual women, providing them with information, training, and support in dealing with job-related problems.

Other information such as sources of funding, national affiliation and meeting schedules are also found in these brochures. Several contain a "Bill of Rights for Office Workers," spelling out more specifically the goals mentioned earlier. All have an attached or enclosed coupon that is used to apply for membership and ask for further information. Photographs of women participating in the organization's events and graphics or cartoons representing office situations are also used in these brochures.

Newsletters make up a large proportion of materials published by local groups and the national organization. Local organizations produce newsletters periodically, depending upon availability of funds and interest on the part of the membership. After a long period without a newsletter at the Baltimore local, in October 1980 a newsletter was once again printed, with 5,000 copies distributed both through mailings and general public distribution. The purpose of the first edition was two-fold—to give information about the group, including attracting new members, and to raise money through a four-page ad supplement. Several hundred dollars were raised with this effort.

An in-depth examination of the national organization and the variety of ways it carries out campaigns, raises funds, publicizes issues, and is tied into local organizations requires further investigation than is furnished in this chapter. I have given this very brief overview in order to provide a general framework from which to examine the experiences and ideas of the membership in one local organization. The remainder of this chapter contains a description of Baltimore Working Women—its history, present structure, and membership. There is a focus on the issues that are important to participants and their motivations for joining.

HISTORY OF BALTIMORE WORKING WOMEN

Baltimore Working Women (BWW), previously known as Women Employed in Baltimore, is a local affiliate of Working Women, National Association of Office Workers. At the time of this study there were 250 paid members with approximately 2,000 people on the organization's mailing list. Interviews with founding members and two of the staff at BWW, including the first staff person hired, enabled me to get a fairly clear-cut picture of the early stages of the organization in Baltimore.

Publicity about groups in other cities, particularly "9 to 5" in Boston (one of the earliest clerical workers' organizations, and now also an affiliate of Working Women) and Women Employed in Chicago (presently not affiliated) piqued the interest of a number of women living and working in Baltimore. An informal group of women, few of whom were clerical workers at that time, were looking for a vehicle to help organize women office workers. These women felt dissatisfied with the already-existing organizations precisely because they did not address issues of clerical workers, but rather concentrated on women in management and professional jobs. That this interest prevailed despite the fact that few of these women were clerical workers themselves was explained by one of the founders. She pointed out that it wasn't necessarily formed for their personal interests, ". . . but we saw ourselves affected by some of the same things as clerical workers." These early members were primarily professional workers in the city government who were feminists. Several held generally left-of-center political views. Though not all were affiliated with the political left, some were members of the New American Movement and described themselves as socialists and socialist-feminists. As one founder expressed it,

> . . . I think that while I've never really been a clerical worker with the exception of just some real short stints, it was mostly for political reasons. I saw it as an important thing to do, to do clerical organizing and help [it] get started . . . I'd been in touch with women who were doing this around the country and was kind of excited by the national movement that was starting and the work that other people had done, and really wanted to try to make use of some of those other contacts to help it get going.

When asked why she felt it was politically important to organize clerical workers, she replied,

> . . . it's such a large segment of the women's work force that are in clerical jobs, and women who are not organized in other ways. Also . . . doing clerical organizing seems to combine a feminist analysis as well as labor issues, because women's roles as secretaries and other clerical workers are pretty unique in the way they see themselves and are seen in the office, and the way they are treated. There's a lot of unfairness that comes a lot from women's role in society as well as from a particular job.

Not all founders shared these views. In fact, in the early stages there was some debate about whether the group should limit itself to clerical workers, or include women workers in all occupations. This conflict was resolved somewhat later when the first staff member was hired. She supported the position of focusing on clerical workers, and that direction has been maintained ever since.

The first public act took the form of a survey of working women in Baltimore, using a questionnaire developed by a clerical workers' organization in Chicago. About 60 women were recruited by word of mouth to distribute 10,000 surveys in downtown Baltimore on National Secretaries' Day in 1978. There was extensive newspaper and television coverage of this activity. Over 700 people responded to the survey. This was considered a surprisingly large response and was interpreted as exemplifying the need for a working women's organization. A group of about 20 people helped compile the data during the summer of 1978. In addition to providing information about the working conditions of Baltimore's office workers, the surveys furnished names and addresses of the respondents, many of whom were subsequently contacted. A considerable number of currently active members first joined after filling out the survey and being invited to attend the first formal general meeting. One long-term participant remembers her introduction to the organization:

> . . . at the moment of filling it out I thought, my God, why wasn't something like this done before, and I scrawled on the bottom I wanted to help and within a day or two I got a call, and I've been helping ever since. I think it's many, many years overdue.

This entire project received assistance from various sources, the main one being the Working Women's Organizing Project, which later became Working Women. On October 5, 1978 the group made a public announcement of the formation of the organization, revealing the findings of the survey. Press coverage was considered excellent. Monthly general meetings have been held ever since.

Another major step towards formalization was the hiring of a full-time staff person, mentioned earlier. A personnel committee of three women was created to evaluate applicants. Two women applied for the job, both of whom had been active in the original group. The decision-making process was left up to the committee. The salary of the first staff person was funded by the Ms Foundation and the Women's Resource and Advocacy Center, which also provided office space for the fledgling organization.

The decision to elect officers was postponed for a year in order to try to involve as many people as possible in the organization before formally selecting more people for leadership roles. This decision was made on the advice of other established organizations in the emerging national network.

As the organization grew, most of those actively involved nonclerical organizers left the group. They had seen their commitment as short term and limited to its early stages. At the same time, the involvement of office workers increased.

GENERAL GOALS

As an affiliate of a large national organization, BWW aligns itself with the goals spelled out by Working Women. In both national and local publications the goal is stated in these general terms: "to gain rights and respect for working women." While this is a slogan for the group as much as it is a goal, it represents a broad approach encompassing the following areas:

1. Providing information about the history, present status, and legal rights of working women, particularly office workers. This is carried out through presentations at meetings and workshops, and by guest speakers and printed information.

2. Outreach to encourage public awareness of the status of working women and the activities of the organization, to attract new membership, and fundraising. Leafleting, press conferences, public forums, and newsletters are most often used to accomplish this.

3. Direct actions designed to affect specific job areas. For instance, through a combination of leafleting, surveying, rallies, and public presentations, BWW won job postings at a large city bank.

4. Providing an arena for gaining organizing skills. Public speaking and participation in large public events help build the confidence needed to become effective as individuals and as a group. Learning how to run a meeting, raise funds, attract membership and run a campaign are all significant skills taught to members, who are anxious to learn such skills. As one active member points out, "This is a wonderful learning organization. If you need to gain leadership skills . . . speech-making . . . fundraising . . . this is a great place to learn."

5. Building solidarity among women office workers by sharing job experiences with others, in the context of the organization. This encourages women to see the benefits of collective effort. Some women point out that this is the first organization they have ever belonged to: "I always wanted to be an individualist, I guess, and didn't want to need an organization, but I found sometimes you do need them." Overall, participants echo the call for solidarity. One active member explains why she joined BWW:

> Because it's working. It's not just a bitch session where everybody sits around and goes, "Oh, this is terrible . . . and why is it like this and somebody ought to do something." The whole attitude is, "What can we do, and how can we do it in the most effective and fastest way? And how can we reach the most amount of people?"

An older woman explained that the organization gives women

> . . . the chance to help us speak for ourselves, which are things we never thought we could do; meeting other women who have perhaps more nerve; meeting the younger women. They have a different attitude. They really do . . . They're honest . . . I've learned a lot from them. I've learned to speak up.

Few question the purpose or direction of activities. Most specific activities are planned in committee meetings and are brought to the general meetings either as information to pass along, to request volunteers to help carry out related tasks, or to request a decision by the general membership through a vote. Issues that are presented as information may include plans for a fundraiser, leafleting of a particular piece of employment or announcement of a press conference. Those issues that are brought before the membership for a vote have included general elections, and changing the name of the group.

Aside from organizational goals, a few participants have mentioned individual goals, including learning job skills and exposure to new job opportunities. An active member explains, ". . . I see it as a way to further my career . . . It's one way to get noticed . . . get on one of these commissions for women."

SPECIFIC GOALS

The national organization works closely with its local affiliates in encouraging activities designed to achieve specific victories within the context of the general goals of winning rights and respect for office workers. Availability of funding and broad national issues generate similar interests from city to city. As a consequence, at the time of this study, almost all local chapters, including BWW had two main foci:* 1) the working conditions of women employed in banks; and 2) age discrimination among all women office workers. Within the context of these two areas, a variety of specific goals were established.

The banking campaign in Baltimore took on the issue of job postings at a large local bank. Equal pay has been an issue in many organizations, and was often directed at banks. The purpose of the focus on banks was based on two important premises. First, banks employ an increasing number of women in menial positions. For instance, over 90 percent of bank tellers are women.[1] Not surprisingly, women hold very few of the managerial positions in banks. A survey conducted by BWW found that starting salaries at a number of banks in Baltimore ranged from $5,600 to $7,390 in 1979, and that most women working in those banks receive salaries below $11,000, regardless of the number of years they have worked there. Clearly, banks would be considered a good target from the standpoint of wanting to improve the working conditions for women. Secondly, the national organization believes that an emphasis on banks is a way of showing that Working Women is able to take on some of the most powerful financial institutions. Karen Nussbaum, head of the national office in

---

*The specific goals described here have changed somewhat since this study was done. By 1982 the organization was focusing on three specific areas: equal pay for comparable worth; health and safety on the job; and reclassification of job titles. According to a staff member, these changes reflect the growth of concern about these issues among office workers.

Cleveland, pointed out in a speech at the Summer School for Working Women in 1980 that winning against the biggest corporate institutions makes office workers aware that change is possible. It also serves to reflect the seriousness of the organization to those in doubt.

The age discrimination campaign was created out of an awareness of the employment problems of women over 40 years old whose numbers in the labor force have been increasing steadily over the years. The purpose of the campaign is described in a report published by Working Women. "We need to put an end to the dual discrimination of age and sex that plagues women over 40, so that women can achieve job satisfaction in their later working years and won't have to look forward to a retirement that becomes a prison of poverty and despair."[2]

In Baltimore, this campaign took the form of a highly successful public forum in which personal testimonies were given and local political leaders lent their support. A group of women in the organization studied the problematic and confusing pension laws in order to pass along information to others as well as to plan actions around discriminatory pension policies. There was an ongoing attempt to attract younger members to this issue who had not given much thought to their own prospects of living in poverty in old age. The general membership seemed receptive to this issue, and some of the younger members have expressed their concern. One woman looked at the disparity between knowledge acquired over the years and low pay at one place of employment:

> I see women down there that have been there 20 to 25 years, and I really don't think they get the prestige for all the knowledge they have . . . they've changed over to a new computer system and all these women have knowledge the old way, but that old way is still instilled within that new system. And they know so much. Everybody is always going to these women and asking them questions, but their pay hasn't been upgraded that much . . . It's really disgusting . . . I'm 26 years old. I'm going to be 40 before I know it. It's going to come up quick, and I don't want to be sitting there and have ten people coming over and asking me all the questions and meanwhile my paycheck is smaller.

Another young woman expressed concern about pensions.

> It scares me. I know how much trouble I have surviving on my regular paycheck, and I think, gosh, if I'm going to have to live on that someday, I'm really going to be in trouble. We're all going to have to live in a big home together somewhere: Office Workers' Home!

Nevertheless, the age committee was made up primarily of women over 40 years old.

There was a plan underway to combine the banking and age discrimination campaigns into a single effort to examine age discrimination in banks, an efficient consolidation of energy that was supported by both committees. The specific focus of the campaign had not been defined as of this writing, though it was expected to involve a case of age discrimination of women employees at a particular bank.

ORGANIZATIONAL STRUCTURE

Membership

Attendance at general monthly meetings has ranged from a low of 20 to a high of 58 during the period of observation from October 1979 to October 1980, with the number averaging in the 30s. Attendance might be affected by the agenda, with higher attendance when there are elections, special presentations, or guest speakers, as well as outside conditions such as weather or competing with Baltimore Oriole's baseball games. According to the organization's records, public events are usually attended by a larger number of people. Public hearings and a booth at the Women's Fair in Baltimore attracted large crowds. Committee meetings, on the other hand, were usually attended by less than ten people.

There is no official account of the membership by race or age. When asked, the staff estimated that approximately one-third of the members are black, with very few other minority groups represented. The age range is from 18 to 60 years old, with the majority of members in their 20s and 30s. These numbers approximate my own estimates based on observations at general meetings.

A survey was distributed at several organizational events, including a general meeting, a rally, and a few committee meetings. Thirty-four questionnaires were completed and returned. While the results are not reflective of the entire membership, they represent those who are most likely to be active and attend events. Tables 3.1–3.4 show the race, age, marital status, and presence of children of the respondents.

TABLE 3.1

Race of Respondents

Race	Number
White	19
Nonwhite	14*
NA	1
Total	34

*Twelve respondents reported their race as black.

TABLE 3.2

Age of Respondents

Age	Number
20–29	13
30–39	9
40–49	4
50 and over	6
NA	2
Total	34

Most of the members did not know each other before joining the organization, although a few have brought friends and co-workers to meetings. When it was first organized, the founding women either knew each other through the workplace or outside political activities in which they shared common interests, but this network no longer plays a significant role for most members. On several occasions, women working for the same company met for the first time at a general meeting, much to their mutual surprise.

I have defined four distinct structural groupings of the membership based on the degree and type of involvement in the organization:

1. *The staff* is composed of two full-time paid workers and one half-time volunteer (a work-study student from a local university), who has been with the organization less than one year. The first staffperson hired has since left her position, having moved to another state, and is presently doing similar work there. She

TABLE 3.3

Marital Status of Respondents

Marital Status	Number
Never married	9
Married	9
Divorced or Separated	9
Living Together or Common–law Marriage	4*
Widowed	2
NA	2
Total	35

*One respondent reported her marital status as divorced and living together, which accounts for the total of 35.

TABLE 3.4

Presence and Age of Children among Respondents

Children	Number
18 or older	11*
7 to 17	7*
6 or under	3
No children	15
NA	2
Total	38

*Three women had children in the categories 18 or older and 7 to 17. Four women had children in the categories 7 to 17 and 6 or under, which accounts for the total of 38.

was replaced in June, 1980 by a woman who had been an active member of the organization. The other full-time staffperson has been with the organization since the spring of 1979. The staff conducts the day-to-day operations of the organization and maintains close communication with the national organization. The three staff members schedule events and meetings, contact potential members, perform most of the office clerical tasks, and work closely with the steering council (made up of elected officers) in planning the general direction of the group as well as specific events. They also participate in committee meetings and thereby influence the direction of campaigns. Their role is seen as advisory, as they are the most informed participants in the organization and act as a liaison between the national organization and the local membership.

2. *Highly active members* are composed of several groups, all of whom share a high level of participation and decision-making power. These are: a) elected officers; b) committee or campaign chairpersons; c) individuals who are regular participants in general meetings, specific campaigns, actions, public speaking, and other activities, but who are neither officers nor chairs on committees. Their high level of participation is measured by the number of activities in which they are involved. The staff estimates there are about 30 such members who fit this description.

3. *Moderately active members* are those who regularly attend meetings but are not involved in other activities on a regular basis, or those who are involved in depth in one specific campaign to the exclusion of any other participation in the group. This category also includes those who are sporadically involved (that is, very active for two months, inactive for three months). According to the staff, there are about 75 such members.

4. *Inactive potentials* are either not yet members, or have recently joined, and have shown sufficient interest in the organization to attend one or two meetings. What percentage of these people go on to become active is difficult to assess, as there is little follow-up. The names of all those attending are put on the mailing

list. It is assumed that a large number of those on the list attend only a few meetings, since the mailing list contained 2,000 names.

Recruitment

A large number of the active members were recruited by the staff following the initial survey in 1978. Most were called and asked to help with mailings or setting up meetings. This is still a common recruitment strategy. Once a woman shows interest in the organization by telephoning about a job problem, attending an event, and getting on the mailing list, or responding to a questionnaire, the staff usually follows up by inviting the woman to participate in an event, particularly to help do some work. Staff members believe this enables the woman to get a sense of the organization while feeling useful. Many members have joked about how they were roped into doing tasks for BWW when they were first recruited. Another tactic used to attract new members is the recruitment luncheon in which a staff person or active member, usually an officer, sets up a lunch meeting with one or more prospective members to discuss their job problems and to describe the organization. This small-group discussion, while time consuming, has proven an effective way to encourage women to join.

The recruitment process is on-going, and there is always pressure to find potential members. Occasionally specific events are set up to draw new participants to the organization. Since both funding and activities rely heavily on membership, recruitment is of central concern to the leadership.

The Setting

There are two main bases of operations for Baltimore's Working Women. The office is located in what might kindly be described as two cozy rooms in the YWCA in the center of town. In fact, it is crowded to overflowing with desks, filing cabinets, office equipment and people, but this is a tremendous improvement over the single room they had until the summer of 1980. Most of the daily staff business is carried out in this office, while the meetings are generally held in the social hall of a nearby church. In contrast, this meeting room is large and comfortable, and could easily accommodate a hundred people. General meetings are held here with participants sitting at six or seven large round tables that facilitate informal discussion before and after meetings. There is a podium at the front of the room from which participants speak. In the rear of the hall, near the entrance, is a sign-up sheet and name tags, which are worn by almost everyone. There are two tables, one with information in the form of brochures, pamphlets, flyers and copies of newspaper clippings about the group. Some articles are free, while others are for sale. The other table usually has cookies or chips and coffee with a donation box for contributions. Generally, people congregate around these two tables before and after meetings to socialize.

The Meetings

During meetings, the staff usually sits in the back, away from the tables, and only participates when asked a specific question or to offer clarification on a particular issue or event. Before and after meetings, however, they mingle with the rest of the participants and are often seen introducing themselves to new people or introducing several people to each other who might share common interests or jobs. Staff persons explained that they deliberately stay in the background during general meetings in order to encourage the full participation of the members. This does not necessarily hold true in smaller committee meetings, where it has been observed that staff members play an active, often leadership role.

Formal participants in meetings, such as the officers, campaign directors, or active members reporting on an event, generally come to the front of the room when they are called upon, and address the group from the podium. Otherwise, they are spread throughout the room. The setting, with the round tables, name tags, food, and encouragement of discussion, does much to engender a friendly atmosphere.

Perhaps the most interesting aspect of the general meetings is the style in which they are conducted. My own observations combined with those of others who often attend meetings, are that there is an air of politeness and consideration that pervades all discussion, formal or informal. There is an effort to include as many people as possible. When asked about this, a staff person who was fairly new to the organization commented that she had observed the same process in other chapters of Working Women, and has assumed that it was a policy developed on the national level before she had arrived. The longest-term staff member explained that it wasn't a deliberate policy, but a natural process that evolved as the organization grew. Whether deliberate or not, it has the effect of creating a nonthreatening, comfortable atmosphere, unlike most highly-structured organizations. A description of a typical meeting will illustrate the predominance of this atmosphere. Shortly after the meeting is called to order by the chair (who often includes a corny but much appreciated original poem about working women), people attending for the first time are asked to introduce themselves and announce where they work. This always generates applause from the others, who are especially delighted when the new person says she works for a bank or large corporation. Throughout the meeting, different people go to the podium to give reports on committee meetings, public events, and, once in a while, personal testimonies about their job experiences. All reports are met with applause when completed. In addition to providing information to the group, it gives the speaker an opportunity to practice public speaking in a nonthreatening situation. Meetings often include a guest speaker or panel presentation on a particular issue of concern to clerical workers. A song may signal the end of the meeting, at which point people meet informally with one another and discuss jobs, family, school, and generally catch up on common interests.

There have been few moments of large-scale dissent or argument, which is partially explained by the fact that the hammering out of decisions usually takes place in committee meetings, after which a package may be brought to the general membership for a vote. In a year of observation, only two incidents of disagreement stand out. One issue involved a decision as to whether or not to have a rotating chair or a permanent chair at the first election. The other concerned the necessity of changing the name of the organization due to legal problems with another group of a similar name. In each case an explanation by the staff sufficed, and the organization agreed to support the suggestions of the staff with little argument. Aside from these two instances, which may serve as examples of power differentials between paid staff and active members (see later discussion on power), general meetings are free from dissent or argument. All this encourages a nonthreatening atmosphere of cooperation and mutual support. As one officer put it, "I like it because there isn't the infighting. I don't always agree with other people . . . but we don't sit there and fight about it . . . We come to some sort of decision."

Aside from general meetings, there are a number of smaller meetings held for a variety of purposes. The two committees, age discrimination and banking, each held monthly meetings during my year of observation. These were attended by one staff person each and six or seven committee members. There is an ongoing attempt to draw more interest from the general membership into committees. The steering council, made up of staff and officers, holds a monthly meeting and periodic evaluation sessions in which the goals and strategies of the organization are discussed.

Most of the decision making of the organization takes place in committee meetings and in the steering council, where information about the national organization is brought by the staff to the participants to help them decide on the direction of the campaigns. When special events are planned, such as National Secretaries' Day, Boss Day, or fundraisers, special committees are formed and meet to plan the event. Periodically, workshops are held as training sessions for leadership skills or for learning about particular issues of concern to clerical workers. Mailing parties are organized when a large mailing of newsletters or announcements of events are anticipated, and these are attended by staff and rank-and-file members, often including new participants who do not seem to mind stuffing envelopes for an organization they know little about.

WHY WOMEN JOIN

The social activities that take place are generated by the shared interest members have in the work experiences of women. This interest can be divided into two main categories related to the particular concerns of those involved. According to interview responses, people usually participate in these activities either because they have specific job problems they wish to solve in the context of the group, or out of a desire to help working women in general. While many participants are interested in both areas, members usually fall into one category or the other.

In the questionnaire distributed to the membership, responses were more varied. When asked why they originally attended meetings, the distribution of responses reflected diverse interests. Many respondents checked more than one response (see Table 3.5). Other responses written in by respondents varied from learning new skills and getting information about the organization, to getting emotional support. The low response rate for the category "Because of specific problem on the job," is puzzling, since later in the survey many respondents described specific job problems that they encountered. Perhaps they did not see those problems as solvable within the organization, but rather felt they could be better served by learning about their rights as workers in general.

Of those who join due to specific job problems, there is widespread awareness that help comes in the form of sharing their experiences with

TABLE 3.5

Respondents' Reasons for Attending Meetings

Reason for Attending	Number
To learn more about my rights as a working woman	26
To help other working women	25
To improve overall working conditions	10
Because of a specific problem on the job	8
To make new friends	8

others who are sympathetic and in structured efforts to confront job inequalities. One newcomer expressed these thoughts:

> I came to the meeting tonight because I work for the city. People always say you can't fight City Hall, but I feel I have some legitimate gripes, and I'm trying to work within City Hall to get something done about them. But because I'm a woman and because they don't take me seriously, I'm just running around in circles. So I want to share my problems with other women. Maybe I could get some help from women who have had the same experience.

Another summarized an attitude couched more in symbolic terms rather than realistic experience, but her thoughts represent the impression many have of the organization:

> I was talking to a couple of the people who came tonight for the first time, and they were saying that they were having problems on their job, and that seems to be the thing that draws people in our organization . . . when it gets to the point where they can't handle it themselves, or the bosses are ganging up on them, and they need somebody to stand behind them, they need to be able to say as I said to my boss, "If you mess with me, I'll have a picket line here in the morning. At 8:30 there will be twenty women marching around outside with signs with your name on it . . ."

Some women expressed a more generalized frustration and isolation as women workers, rather than experiencing specific problems. They felt the need to associate with other women in similar positions:

> I've really found it to be a good experience [to] meet other people that are involved, interested in the same thing, 'cause sometimes I know at work where I am, girls don't seem to be too much into that. I used to think I was the only person who even thought about it. It makes you feel that you're not alone.

This need for a community of people who share similar experiences is further explained by another participant, "I feel that coming to these meetings has made me feel better and I'm trying to get people I work with to get involved, but it's hard. It's hard because even some of the women I work with don't take it seriously."

Not surprisingly, some of the most actively involved members joined for more altruistic reasons. In fact, when asked about their jobs, they explained that they had no problems at work, some of which were administrative or high level secretarial positions. Several described their participation as fulfilling a desire to help other women. One nonclerical member explained:

> I still see some of the duties I do as somewhat clerical. But I just feel a commitment to this organization. Most of the women I know are in clerical work. Most of the women in the world are in clerical work. And I just think it's fine to want to promote women into upward mobility jobs, management jobs, and I think that's a nice goal, but I don't see that you're going to mainstream every employee into a management level. You're always going to have your peons. I think if you raise the standard of living, some of the benefits for a bigger mass of people, you're doing a more beneficial thing than to get three people vice-presidentships.

One officer explained that she felt a certain obligation to help other women, partly because she was not in a position to be fired if it was discovered that she was actively involved. She further explained her interest in a working women's organization:

> I always felt very sympathetic to women. Women have been the nicest people I have known, and they're very responsible. A lot of things happen to them. After I broke [from my marriage] I had a hard time getting credit and a lot of things like that. So when the initial survey came out a couple of years ago, I filled it out . . . I wrote on there "If you can use my help, I'll help a little bit at a time." And as I got involved I just saw that there was a real need there for me, and I felt that I was going to do something . . . I really care about people.

The flip side of the officer's desire to help from the position of her secure, well-paid job, was the motivation of the feisty former bank clerk who described her first involvement with BWW this way:

> . . . the vice-president told everybody not to answer the survey, and if they were caught, they would be fired. So I called up [BWW] . . . and asked if I could come and pick up twenty or thirty surveys during my lunch hour . . . I think what you do on your own time is your business, and I felt that he had no right to tell the employees that.

While this is not a position taken by all of the participants, it does exemplify the willingness to take risks if the effort is considered worthwhile, either from the standpoint of improving one's own work situation or in an attempt to help others.

The interests shared by these women as they join the organization are the seeds of the solidarity so necessary to the collective efforts of the group as a whole.

THE POWER STRUCTURE

Understanding the power relations in BWW is complex, as it contains a combination of formalized power found in the staff, and a somewhat different type of formal power among the elected officers. There are also the democratic procedures of the general meetings and committee meetings that at some times appear formal and at others not. What further complicates, but partly explains, these power dynamics is BWW's relationship to the national organization, Working Women.

Decisions concerning the programs of the organization as a whole are derived from the National Board, which is comprised of representatives from local groups and one national staff member. Generally, the program director of the national staff distributes proposals to the locals prior to the board meetings. These are then discussed among the locals prior to sending representatives to the meeting. National programs develop out of the priorities set by the National Board. Since the Board is composed almost entirely of local members this insures that national programs are compatible with local interests. While interests are compatible in general, some conflict may arise concerning specific use of funds, as grant proposals do not always reflect the exact interests of a given local group. A significant portion of local funding comes from the national organization which, in turn, gets most of its money from large foundations. Consequently, the money sent to local affiliates is often designated prior to its arrival to be spent on particular projects as specified in the grant proposals. The following is an example of how this can affect the decision-making process at the local level.

The BWW Age Committee had been planning to do a survey of older working women in order to present information to the public, and to carry out an action at a targeted company. At a committee meeting in which this was to be discussed, a staff member explained to the group that there would be greater availability of funds from the national organization if the original project was scratched in favor of a somewhat different, although not incompatible one. There was much discussion involving the source of funding and the use for which it was designated by the constraints on the grant, along with an explanation of how badly BWW needed the money. The Age Committee was convinced, and thus voted to change the direction of the project to fit the requirements of the funding.

The staff influences members but also supports whatever decisions the committee makes. It is, in effect, beholden both to the national office and to the general membership of the local organization. The membership appeared quite willing to go along with the staff's suggestion concerning the project, and thus conflict was averted. Furthermore, it was agreed that the committee would present this decision to the general membership. There was a discussion concerning whether or not the general membership should vote on this issue, and it was decided that the committee's decision was sufficient.

It is apparent that there is no formal procedure for making these kinds of decisions, despite the distinctions of power between the staff, elected officers and rank-and-file members. The availability of funds for various activities plays a major role in the decision to pursue certain projects, although there is a considerable amount of leeway within projects in which to meet goals. The membership does not seem to begrudge the staff or the national office the right to decide the general direction of the organization, probably for the simple reason that the goals of all involved are at this point basically the same. Those who do not share these goals do not participate for long. Those active in the organization realize that funds often come from outside sources for specific purposes and cannot be reassigned to other projects. It is unlikely that most of the members, even relatively active ones, fully understand the relationship of the organization to the national office, nor the roles the staff plays between the two groups.

SPECIFIC ACTIONS

Perhaps one of the most interesting aspects of the organization is found in its approach to specific actions. Since Baltimore Working Women is a city-based group, rather than oriented toward one workplace, it tries to address the most far-reaching issues for women office workers. A particular campaign aimed at a large bank may not have direct impact on the working conditions of any one member of the organization, unless that woman happens to work at that bank. Therefore, the approach to issues forces activists to relate to the problem of women office workers in a broad sense. National occasions such as National Secretaries' Day and Boss Day provide vehicles through which the group can announce a given campaign while trying to tie it in with the problems faced by the majority of its constituency and potential constituency. These activities also serve the purpose of raising consciousness.

Observations of specific actions, particularly mass rallies, indicate a high level of enthusiasm among a sizeable stable number of participants. Officers are almost always present as well as a cross section of the active rank-and-file members. Usually a few of the newest members are given small roles to play or tasks to perform in order to encourage them to participate. While most participants in these events felt jittery about being in the public eye, this was most often due to general nervousness of having to perform in public, rather than fear of being seen by their bosses and suffering retribution. Those who had such fears usually did not openly participate in public events. One incident was reported in which a picture of a rally participant appeared in the newspaper. She was subsequently threatened with being fired from her job. Many other members do not try to hide their participation from their employers. Usually the women reported that if their bosses did see them, the result was good-natured teasing. Nevertheless, some women did not find this a relief: "I think a lot of the men in my office are amused at my antics. They see me leafleting on the street. They sort of have a tongue-in-cheek attitude, and I really feel we're going to have to bring more pressure to bear."

Successful campaigns have been built around broad issues that are believed to affect women office workers. The first step involves publicizing an event by leafleting on busy downtown streets announcing a campaign. If a particular institution is being approached, the publicity involves informing as many employees of that institution as possible through the leaflets. The campaign is then publicly announced at a rally and the mass media is relied upon to further increase knowledge about it.

Actions almost always involve colorful skits with amateur but effective acting on the part of members as well as information presented in a serious manner. These sorts of events inevitably catch the eye of the mass media, an important aspect of any public event. The organization has found that public embarrassment of an official of a company both helps get publicity for the campaigns into the media as well as forces the institution to deal with the issues. A good example was the presentation of the "Miser of the Year" award given to a distinguished bank president. The campaign addressed the issue of lack of job postings for the bank's clerical staff to apply for promotional opportunities. The president of the bank responded to the action with anger, yet his relatively quick response to charges by the organization indicated that he was not interested in furthering his image as a miser. Since many large companies are sensitive to adverse publicity, this is seen as an effective technique.

Other actions are less dramatic, but of equal significance. A campaign concerning older working women was kicked off with a press conference in which younger women read the testimonies of their older counterparts to a room full of reporters. In this case, the women whose experiences were being recounted did, in fact, fear losing their jobs and decided to protect their anonymity by having others read their stories.

Campaigns have also involved less public actions such as getting the appropriate government agency to investigate a given workplace concerning issues such as sex or age discrimination in pay or promotions. Almost all campaigns have educational and consciousness-raising goals involving specific issues such as information about pension systems or how to file discrimination charges with government agencies. Other educational goals involve workshops on the history of women workers and practical lessons on leadership, speechmaking, and running campaigns. While these last areas mentioned are primarily in-house activities, they are part of the overall format encouraging the raising of consciousness and more public activism of the members.

One important aspect of activism is understanding how the participants themselves feel about it. Most are enthusiastic about public actions, but often need encouragement to participate, as few have ever given speeches or sung in public before. Most reported that they like the style of actions taken by the group, and often compare it to the lack of actions taken elsewhere, particularly in their own workplaces. One activist expressed frustration with her co-workers' lack of interest in job actions:

> . . . I think a lot of women feel defeated. Women in my office say to me—I'm the only member, and we have, what, sixty or seventy secretaries—They say to me, "What can we do? What can we do? You can't do anything. There's nothing you can do about it. Why are you trying so hard? You're not going to be able to do anything." I'm not built that way. I think the office is not militant enough. If we did hang together we could do something. I know trying to bring the union into my firm would be absolutely hopeless. Many of the young girls, they laugh at me. They'll say to me, "Oh shut up, _____," or "There goes _____ again. Why doesn't she shut up."

When asked what they thought of the organization, most women indicated in a general fashion that they liked the idea that large numbers of women could accomplish improved working conditions through collective action:

> I think it's really important that we realize that our strength is in numbers and because we're women we can accomplish things. . . . I don't think we've had the kind of control that we should have. I think it's just now that we're realizing—feeling our oats—and we can go and do these things for ourselves . . .

While no one mentioned actions any more militant than those already tried, several indicated that increased militance was appropriate:

> . . . I feel that whatever can be done to stop the treatment that we're getting, should be done. I think we deserve the same kind of respect and treatment that the men feel they're entitled to. We're just as entitled, and I feel we've got to hang on, and we've got to do whatever we can to accomplish this.

PERSONAL DEVELOPMENT AMONG
ORGANIZATION MEMBERS

It is important to observe mass actions, rallies, press conferences, meetings, and increases in activism of members, but there are also very important changes that take place on a personal, individual level, as reported by the respondents. Personal growth entails learning new skills (chairing, public speaking, writing, and so on), becoming familiar with legal rights, and experiencing solidarity with other women in an otherwise isolating sex/occupational category. These personal developments do not fit in with classical work literature if one tries to comprehend their contribution to a workers' movement. Yet if one examines feminist literature, the theme, "the personal is political" is found. Interviews with participants reveal that there is a reciprocal relationship between personal growth and increased public activism to improve working conditions. The two experiences act on each other progressively so that as a woman becomes more active, she experiences a growth in confidence, which furthers her involvement in the group and so forth. The concrete effects of this as reported in interviews are a combination of actual improvements of work conditions for individual women either through confrontations with one's employer or finding a new and better job, as well as successful campaigns sponsored by the group as a whole, which may or may not affect individual members directly. The success of a campaign relies equally upon the specifics of the action as well as the confidence and knowledge of the individuals involved.

When asked in interviews if they had experienced any personal changes since joining the organization, respondents almost uniformly reported that their self-confidence had increased. This was accomplished in several ways. Some members found themselves in the public eye performing specific skills, such as chairing meetings or speaking at public events, often in front of television cameras. The former chair of the organization, who by all accounts appears extremely self-confident in public, explained her experiences:

> I don't particularly care for chairing. I'm a bashful person. It's very painful for me to do that, to get up and talk . . . You should have been to the press conference. It was terrible and I was really intimidated. My first big speaking thing. They get you slowly into that, too. Like they have you chair a meeting, then it works up . . . but I did it by practicing. I figure I'm going to do it so why get up there, why act silly. Just try to overcome it.

Another active woman described her experience at an event where Jane

Fonda was speaking. Fifteen hundred people attended and the media was there in full force:

> . . . Jane Fonda leaned over one time and tapped my knee while we were on the platform and said, "Are you scared?" and I said, "Of course, I've never done anything like this in my life." But at least I had the opportunity to do it and I'd like to see more women find that they can do it if they have to.

Even less auspicious events challenge the fears of these women and build their confidence. One woman describes the first time she leafleted, one of the most common activities carried out by the organization. "I was nervous about doing that, and after a while I was disappointed when everybody practically left and took their bus home 'cause I had had a ball. It gets to be friendly." Overall, participation in public events gives these women the opportunity to express themselves in ways not otherwise available to them:

> I know it's done a world of good for me . . . in the public hearing, giving a speech, working with the other women, I saw more creativity come out and more good ideas. It was very nice. I'm very bored in my job so it was very nice to get some outside stimulation in this activity.

Several women expressed feelings that the building of confidence and support from other members make them more optimistic about their futures. "I would like to say that for many, many years I felt hopeless. For the first time in my life I feel that I'm fighting back. It's a great feeling. I have all these women standing behind me." Sharing common experiences with other women affects their responses to problems. ". . . when something happens that I don't like, I can talk about it with someone else and feel that I'm not being just petty, especially if other women are voicing the same complaint . . . I don't have to just sit there and take a thing because they say you do it or else." And: "I'm more willing to speak what's on my mind. . . . I have more confidence. I'm more willing to speak out on something that I think is wrong now. I don't have to simmer with it inside myself and get mad about it." This building of self-confidence is especially important given the lack of recognition most of these women experience for the work they do:

> I found that I have a better feeling about what I do now. It's like before, even I was taking myself for granted. I just thought I was being dictated to. "Do this. Do that. This has to go out now." Now I feel like I'm needed even though nobody says that I am . . . An example of that was that someone was out. The whole office fell apart—the chief's secretary—

the whole thing. Nobody knew what to do, and that made me realize—
Hey! So I think that helps a lot. The way you feel. It will make you be
assertive even when you feel that you aren't. Like in an interview, when
you're a nervous wreck and you walk out and you find you have it. So
that's the way I feel because that has a lot to do with it too, how you feel
about what you're doing.

In addition to the obvious benefits to the organization, this building
of self-confidence has led to concrete changes in the work life of several
women. One woman describes how her new confidence led to new relations with her employer:

> . . . it has helped raise my self-esteem a little bit because you get a lot of
> feedback here and you realize you sit there on the job and you think
> you're doing a great job and you have a lot of responsibility, but you're
> called a clerk, which is demeaning. It's a demeaning title . . . I don't
> mind being called a clerk because I know within myself that the work I
> do is very responsible. I have a hell of a lot of responsibility. I have to
> talk to managers, cashiers, do correspondence, and know how to handle
> myself in certain situations, some that are harassing. Here I am called a
> little clerk and this has helped me to raise my self-esteem . . . I've also
> been rather assertive on my jobs—but I've become even more so. I got
> pressured once. One of my bosses wanted me to tackle two jobs at one
> time without getting more pay. And I just laid down the law and I told
> my boss, "You can tell your boss I'm not doing it." I said if he wants to
> give me two jobs to do, I want to see two paychecks. And I said I know
> he can't force me to do these jobs because that's not what I was hired for.
> And when you come to these meetings and you become part of it, and
> become part of the committees and, like the public hearing, it reinforces
> me and gives me the guts to go and say to my boss, "I'm not going to do
> it. And I want more money." I want more respect and there's not a
> damn thing they can do to me. They can't touch me.

Another describes how her new self-confidence led to a new job:

> I guess it's because of Women Employed [former name] that I took a
> stand while I was working at _____ . I
> thought there was a principle involved and I think because I felt I had
> the support of this organization, that I went ahead and did what I did,
> and that was resigning. Of course, I'm in a new job now with which I'm
> not that happy, but I think it is a challenge, and I feel if I can really just
> hang in there, it just might work out. But I think it's the fact that I did
> belong to this organization that kind of prompted me to resign because
> of this so-called principle and I guess I should feel happy about that,
> which I guess I do.

And yet another explains how specific knowledge gained through the organization will help her select her next job:

> . . . it's given me incentive to know that the next move I make I'll know how to analyze the company better. How to look for things. How to rate their employee turnover, and the number of women they have working and the number of positions. Things that I really wouldn't have thought of before. There's questions that I'll want to ask on my interview. I won't want to just sit there and be asked questions. . . . One major thing is where do women stand regarding the upper positions in the organization and their chance for promotions as well. Just in that alone, it's given me a lot of incentive for my future, and future interviews, making sure that I get to a better position than I'm in now.

It is apparent from these reports that involvement in the organization has had a profound effect on the personal development of the women involved both on concrete levels as experienced in job-related problem solutions as well as on a more subtle abstract level, the growth of confidence and self-esteem. And, of course, these developments increase the effectiveness of the organization that relies on public contact for much of its success. A staff member reflects on the importance of this relationship:

> . . . it's really interesting to look back and see individuals who, the first time I met them I really thought, this person just isn't interested, or she won't feel she's capable enough to get involved in anything . . . Seeing her come out and taking roles, and I guess the leadership development is the other thing . . . that I really like. Women are a lot more capable than they realize 'cause often times their jobs don't utilize what they have to offer. And Women Employed in Baltimore [former name] does, and needs that. We can't function without it.

CONCLUSION

In summary, the organization in this study is part of a growing national network whose goals reflect the interests of women office workers, who are its main base of support. The general goals of "rights and respect for working women" are carried out in a variety of educational projects, media events, rallies, and specific campaigns of direct action aimed primarily at the issues of sex discrimination in banks and the problems of older working women. The process by which campaigns are chosen, projects are developed, and membership is brought together is carried out by the staff, elected officials, and rank-and-file participants in a variety of meeting settings, with the help of the national organization. This process also provides opportunities for personal growth for individual members and the development of solidarity among the membership. The result is a collective effort, with often successful campaigns aimed at specific companies to improve working conditions and provide growth in knowledge about legal rights and working conditions, development of particular organizing skills, and collective support in the form of solidarity.

The structure of Baltimore Working Women, as described in this chapter, of course, cannot stand alone. It relies on its membership who share common work experiences and believe in the necessity of a collective effort to improve working conditions. The following two chapters examine in detail the specific work dissatisfactions experienced by the participants and the types of consciousness that have arisen in the world of the activist woman office worker.

NOTES

1. U.S. Department of Labor, Bureau of Labor Statistics, *U.S. Working Women: A Databook* (Washington, D.C., Government Printing Office Bulletin, 1977), p. 9.

2. Karen Nussbaum, quoted in Working Women, National Association of Office Workers, *Vanished Dreams: Age Discrimination and the Older Woman Worker* (Cleveland, Ohio: Working Women, National Association of Office Workers, 1980).

Chapter 4

Work Dissatisfaction among Clerical Workers: Structural Roots and Present Manifestations

In order to understand the dissatisfactions women experience as clerical workers, we must first examine those structural conditions of the economy and the personal motivations that have led women to work for pay outside the home as these conditions may affect job satisfaction.

STRUCTURAL CONDITIONS

The history of the expansion and feminization of the clerical workforce has already been discussed. We know that for some time the clerical and service industries have been the fastest growing sectors in the economy. We also know that women make up the bulk of those working in these sectors, particularly in the lower-paying menial positions. "Now with more clerical workers, it's important for companies to save on each clerical salary . . . most office workers are now women, and employers are accustomed to using women as a source of cheap labor."[1]

While this expansion has been carried on for some time, it has special significance during periods of economic instability that are accompanied by high rates of unemployment.[2] ". . . The question of whether women are being pulled into the labor force by the new openings in services, clerical posts, or the like, cannot be divorced from the fact that economic pressures push them into the labor market more frequently during periods of economic stagnation."[3] Furthermore, since many of these women are married to men in blue-collar occupations, we must consider that the earnings of those men are at their highest early in their lives, but become insufficient later, when their families' economic needs are the greatest.[4] Thus, women are often pressured to enter the workforce when the financial stability of their families are in jeopardy, due to layoffs, or when their husbands' salaries are too low to meet their economic needs. We know that there has been a tremendous increase in the number of working wives, particularly those with young children, a previously small proportion of women in the labor force.[5] As these women enter the labor force, those already working are also affected by this rapid increase in the availability of cheap labor. One member of Baltimore Working Women recalls this condition as a personal experience.

> I came out of school in 1943 . . . and I worked in a factory in the office, and the neighborhood people who had worked there all their lives suddenly would just be dismissed, and they'd bring in young people, and naturally they could start them at a very low salary, and the older people missed out . . . and so now I'm further along in years and I see the same thing happening . . . They bring in a young girl who will say, "Oh, the job is just wonderful," start her at a very low salary and there you are, you're out the door.

This condition also applies to the rapidly-growing group of women who are single heads of household, either divorced, separated, widowed, or never married, many of whom have dependent children. For them, these conditions are even more severe, as they have no other income to rely upon in addition to their own. Of the women surveyed in Baltimore Working Women, over half reported that they alone provided 100 percent of their family income. An additional 13 percent provided between 75 to 90 percent of their family income. Only 22 percent reported that they provided 50 percent or less.

The increase of women in the workforce has additional economic ramifications from the perspective of consumerism. Specifically, more consumer items can be bought when the family income rises. In fact, if a woman works, she may find she needs to purchase clothes, transportation, childcare, and household items that lessen the time spent in domestic work.[6] So it is also to the economic advantage of big business to put women in a position to increase their consumer purchases.

Other structural conditions that have affected the increase in women working pertain to the lives of modern women and the conditions of the modern household. The combination of a decline in fertility and increased life expectancy gives a woman many more years in which she is free to participate in the workforce. Increased education also contributes to the likelihood that women will work outside the home. The creation of modern appliances and convenience foods free many women from time spent in household tasks.[7]

It appears, then, that structural conditions that encourage women to enter the workforce do so primarily because there is a need for their labor.

Yet there are restrictions due to the type of work available and the potential rewards of that work. There is not much choice as to whether to work or what kind of work a woman might choose. In other words, we are not talking about options for career development, but rather, a very narrow conception of what is considered acceptable work in the context of the needs of the prevailing economic system. Since options are limited in this way, we can expect that many workers will be dissatisfied by those limits if they do not meet economic, personal, or other social needs.

PERSONAL MOTIVATIONS

An understanding of women's motivations for working for pay is complicated by the intricacy of the relationship between their roles in their families, the demands of the workplace, and the economic necessity of working. Both ideologically and pragmatically, family conditions, particularly marital status and presence of children, affect a woman's decision to work, the type of work she will seek, the type of work that will be available to her, and the length of time she will work. Also affected are her attitudes about the purpose of work, the attitudes of her employer towards her position as a worker, and the working conditions she will encounter. Much of the literature supports the belief that ideologically both employers and female employees believe

> . . . that their primary role is that of housewife and mother and that, while they may perchance work, their contribution will be merely supplemental and temporary; they will not have a career. This is true despite the fact that most women who work are essential to support themselves and their families . . .[8]

Furthermore, this ideology functions to force women to accept undesirable working conditions, a decided advantage from the point of view of the employer.

> Where it is to the system's advantage to bludgeon women about their traditional role is that it helps to keep them from demanding too much from work. The female employee must continue to look on her work as secondary, contingent, a luxury for the budget and a privilege for her.[9]

What I found among the respondents in this study reveals a somewhat more complicated situation. Most of the women I interviewed indicated that they worked out of economic necessity that was tied to their family roles. They did not view their earnings as supplemental to the degree that the literature indicates. Among nonmarried respondents, working for a living was an unquestioned assumption. "I need to eat. I need to pay my rent. I've always planned on working. It's not something I've had to decide. Just always knew I was going to work." Many of these women expressed the desire to be independent of husbands or future husbands and saw working as a way to maintain that independence:

> I'm out there making my money because there are things I want to do. I'm not going to be the little household pet to be kept. Sure, maybe one day I'd get married, who knows, but I'd never give up my own money. That's just ridiculous. I would never be on the handout end. I've seen too many women go through that.

Even though they may not see their work as temporary or supplemental, work patterns may still reflect that ideology.

> Women have been socialized to play submissive roles in which their career motivations are stunted and marriage is the dominant goal. They have been deflected from career preparation at almost every level in the educational system by counselors who hold traditional views of sex roles. Eventually they are drawn to clerical work, where both low and high levels of education can be marketed, and where the demands of the job do not threaten to disrupt marital obligations as more challenging work might do.[10]

An older woman whose work patterns reflect her role first as an unmarried daughter and then as wife and mother dropped in and out of the workforce over the years:

> I wasn't there [home] when I worked fulltime. I wasn't coming home and cooking meals the way I used to. People had to pitch in and I had some long faces. When you work fulltime you still do it all. Maybe they'll cook the dinners, but you still do the shopping, the food shopping. You still clean the house.

She returned to the workforce because, as she explained it, "I wanted some money for myself. My husband was very controlling, and this was mine . . ." Even though she felt the need for independence, her erratic, yet typical, work pattern left her unprepared for a career. Instead, she has held a series of clerical jobs, some of which required skills she had not practiced for years, thus increasing the potential for failure. Now divorced, she finds herself financially strapped and often unemployed.

One young clerical worker speculated about whether she would work if she had children. The decision was based not only on her family responsibilities but, significantly, on the type of job she would be holding at the time:

> If I had small children, I may stay home, depending on how I felt . . . If it's something you really want to do, there's nothing wrong with staying home . . . If I had a job where I am now — if I were married now and having a baby — I wouldn't hesitate to take leave of absence and stay home. But if I had a high level job I would think very carefully before doing it.

In other words, the nature of the work available to most women discourages continuity. There is no particular reason to make a lifetime commitment to unpleasant unrewarding work, if one can avoid it. Another woman, a widow, also experienced the rift between the necessity of working and the ideology that leaves women unprepared for anything but low-paying menial work:

> My husband died and there was no money at all; there was no money left. And I worked temporarily, which wasn't a good idea. I should have jumped right in . . . but people said . . . this would be perfect because you can get an idea, build up your skills . . . but that was a long waste of time, no pension situation or anything like that . . .

The widespread use of temporary work among women perhaps best represents the transitory nature of women's work patterns and the ideology of work as secondary to family roles. Most women who do temporary work are either entering the workforce for the first time or reentering after a significant period of absence. It is seen as a way to get work experience and brush up on rusty skills.[11] It is often underpaid menial work, with few benefits due to its temporary nature. By definition, there is low job security. It offers many advantages to the employer, for whom it is essentially more economical.[12] With all its disadvantages to the workers themselves, in the context of the prevailing limited work opportunities for women ". . . the temporary services worker finds variety and a chance for individualism that women in other pursuits may not."[13] One young woman who had worked both factory and clerical jobs explained this advantage to temporary work: ". . . Once you get tired or bored being in one place, or hostile, you know you're going to leave that place . . . You're not bound by their rules and regulations either. You can come in late and leave earlier . . ." In other words, temporary work can be used to make the best of a bad situation, given the general conditions of clerical work. In essence, the popularity of temporary work represents the work patterns and skill levels of many women, providing them with a reentry system for which they are rewarded with low pay, boring work, and job insecurity. Yet since many women argue that clerical work in general often has those same characteristics, if one does temporary work, at least there is some variety and some opportunity to bend regulations.

We can conclude that while women work out of economic necessity, their work patterns are affected by several factors: the ideology that women's primary responsibility is in the home, the degree of economic need, the desire for economic independence, and the undesirability of the work itself. These seemingly contradictory factors work to place women in a specific work circumstance. Need for money and desire for independence encourage women to work, but the nature of the work available and the ideological view encouraging women to see themselves first as wives and mothers, push them into the very type of work that is least secure, lowest paying and most menial. This keeps them in a position as cheap labor available in times of economic crisis as well as tied to traditional patriarchal family relationships, since real financial independence is not achievable in this type of work.

HISTORICAL ORIGINS OF DISSATISFACTION IN CLERICAL WORK

We have already discussed the relationship of the feminization of the clerical workforce to the economic interests of big business, but we must also look at what this shift meant in terms of the prestige of office work. Traditionally, there were always mixed feelings particularly on the part of the blue-collar workforce in terms of the position of the clerk when it was a male-dominated occupation. The clerk himself had pretentions of being middle class, with a strong identification with management. After all, the job required a relatively high level of education, the workplace was clean, one worked with one's head, not hands, and the clerk had a personal relationship with his boss.[14] Nevertheless, there was always some question as to which class the clerk really belonged. Lockwood describes the historical position of the male blackcoated worker in England:

> In terms of social background, education, working conditions, proximity to authority and opportunity of upward mobility, clerks can still perhaps claim a higher status than most manual workers. In terms of productive contribution, income skill, masculinity and group loyalty, they may be accorded a lower status, especially by manual workers themselves . . .[15]

This apparent contradiction in class and status was resolved once women came to dominate the field. The position of clerk has lost its ties to management and its pretentions to prestige. Again, Lockwood:

> This work which already carried the stigma of being 'unmasculine' was one of the first middle-class occupations to become a feminine preserve

of employment. 'Born a man, died a clerk' took on an added social significance as a result. The influx of women merely strengthened the popular stereotype of the clerk and further detracted from the prestige of the occupation. The effect of a high proportion of women in an occupation on the social status of that occupation is a function of the general status of women in society. And here the relationships of sexual inequality within the family have been duplicated in the relationships of sexual inequality in the occupational world. The kinds of work to which women were confined by physical, customary and family limitation were, for the most part, badly paid and poorly regarded. The more the work called for sheer muscular power the less was the threat of female competition; and hence the strong value placed on 'manliness' by such workers. At the other extreme, professional work was generally protected from feminization by the expense and length of training necessary for entry as well as by conventional barriers. As a consequence, 'women's work' came to connote work which required neither superior masculine strength nor superior masculine intellect. On both accounts its prestige was low. When women began to pour into these jobs which required neither manual strength nor prolonged training . . . it was well nigh inevitable that these occupations should suffer a fall in status.[16]

Feminization of clerical work was only one factor in the lowering of the prestige of office work. At the same time, the expansion of the office necessitated a change in the organization of the work process itself, and these changes too led to greater dissatisfaction with the work. Specifically, the mechanization of the office had several effects. It further separated clerical work from management and at the same time brought it closer to manual work. Mechanization and later computerization involved creating specialized tasks which sped up the work process by simplifying and routinizing the work, also enabling greater control over the work process by management.

> . . . it gives management more control over the whole organization, and the chance to make more of a profit . . . If each worker is doing only one task, the supervisor can control the work more completely. It's easy to *measure* how much work people are doing, and set standards to force them to work faster.[17]

This in turn led to offices being organized similarly to factory assembly lines, and workers who responded to their job situation like factory workers.[18] In fact, the reorganization of the office has led to a physical resemblance to factories with typing pools and large rooms filled with sophisticated machinery, where workers stay in one place performing their specialized routine tasks.[19]

There have been two seemingly contradictory trends in clerical work. The increased size and complexity of organizations mean that internal control, coordination and communications become increasingly critical for organizational survival. Since these activities rely largely on clerical labor, clerical work takes on a more central role in the economy. But while clerical work has become more important, organizations have pushed toward streamlining and mechanizing the work to increase efficiency in and control over the work process. This has degraded the work, caused the status of clerical workers to fall, and further restricted opportunities for advancement.[20]

In addition, the reduction of the mental aspect of clerical work to routinized specialized tasks itself seemingly became a justification for low pay.[21]

In sum, the historical forces that may lead to increased job dissatisfaction among clericals derive from the feminization and the mechanization of the office. This contributes to lower pay, lower status, depersonalization of the workplace, deskilling, and little chance for promotion.

Dissatisfaction becomes even more likely since many women are prepared for secretarial work with quite different expectations. There are still some vestiges of the small office with the private secretary, and work organized in this fashion may be highly satisfying.

In secretarial schools women are trained to establish their own procedures and organize their offices. But experts advise companies to standardize and routinize, to apply uniform systems and procedures in every department. They leave less and less room for initiative, even on the part of the lower level executives, not to mention secretaries.[22]

Hence, the disparity between expectations and the reality of the modern office itself may lead to dissatisfaction among clerical workers.

FINDINGS OF THE PRESENT STUDY

This study addressed the issue of job dissatisfaction through the use of a survey questionnaire and in-depth interviews.[23] When asked if they were satisfied with their jobs, the participants in the survey reported the following, shown in Table 4.1. The respondents in this study could not be considered representative of all women office workers, given the source of my sample. Operating on the assumption that most of the women who join Baltimore Working Women are more likely to be dissatisfied with their jobs than clerical workers in general, the research focused not on the degree of dissatisfaction, but the type of dissatisfaction experienced and the contexts in which it occurred.

TABLE 4.1

Job Satisfaction Among Respondents

Degree of Satisfaction	Number
Not at all satisfied	7
Not too satisfied	10
Somewhat satisfied	12
Very satisfied	3
No answer	2
Total	34

When asked in the same survey to indicate the most important issues for working women, these respondents ranked pay, promotions, training programs, and respect as the most crucial. Other high-ranking issues were job security, benefits, race discrimination, and sexual harassment. All of these issues reflect the present low status, degraded position of office workers. Since this organization is directed towards awareness of these issues, it should be expected that the membership reflects those same concerns more than the general population of office workers.

Through open-ended interviews, respondents were asked to describe their jobs and explain what they liked and did not like about their work. Information was also gathered from group discussions and a survey done by the organization itself in 1978. Several distinct, but overlapping categories emerged. There were two fundamental areas of concern, the first of which involves such issues as pay, promotions, work drudgery, and working knowledge. These issues, which will be discussed in detail, fall into the category of *working conditions*. The second category, *work relations*, includes the issues of relations with co-workers and relations with employers, within which we find concerns such as respect, sexual harassment, and other forms of intimidation. While both categories represent working conditions per se, they are grouped in this way in order to distinguish between those conditions having to do with concrete aspects of the work and those having to do with social interaction between the worker and significant people in her work environment.

Working Conditions

Within this category of working conditions, we find two subcategories. The first includes issues of pay and promotions, often intertwined, which relate directly to the measurable productive value of the worker. While low pay characterizes clerical work in general, lack of promotion ensures that salaries remain inadequate, regardless of years spent on the job or skill level. Baltimore Working Women consistently refers to low pay as one of the most significant problems faced by women office workers, and its theme is raised consistently at meetings, in newsletters, at public hearings and mass actions. Reported annual income in this group with few exceptions ranged between $6,000 and $20,000, with over two-thirds reporting earnings between $10,000 and $15,000. This included most of the women whose families depended entirely on that income. Not surprisingly, when asked which issues were considered the most important issues for working women, the respondents in the questionnaire chose pay as the most important, followed closely by promotions. One-fourth of the respondents indicated that they personally experience problems with pay at their present job, and another quarter experience problems related to promotions. Considering that a high proportion of these women are sole breadwinners with dependent children, these issues are of immediate concern. Even among women who considered their pay adequate, the overall salary scale for clericals was restrictive. One woman who likes the salary she gets from a large corporation said, "I might want to change and I really can't afford that change because practically anywhere else I go, any small business, I'm just not going to get paid what I feel I'm worth." Others who liked the wages they received expressed dissatisfaction with the disparity between their wages and those of men in similar positions. "We have men at the company whose titles are 'technician.' Though they do not actually do any typing (although some can type) or take dictation, they do many other similar duties as we 'secretarial-stenographers' and are at LEAST five grades HIGHER!"

Women who receive low wages believe that the way out of this dilemma should be through promotions, but this path is generally blocked. Given the historical expansion of the office, we find a greater number of clericals looking for openings in a few managerial posts.[24] Furthermore, the organization of the modern office has contributed to an even greater separation between the two. The increased specialization and deskilling of office work has favored a separation of traditional white-collar work into the two areas of mental and manual labor usually associated with industrial production.[25]

> Most companies are organized in a way that makes promotion difficult. A clerical worker in a large modern office rarely has the chance to get to know people in management. And typing information on forms all day probably doesn't prepare her for any other job. Besides, most higher-level employees are recruited from outside the firm — usually college-educated white males. Few companies regularly post job openings, and many require employees to make transfer requests through their supervisors, which effectively discourages job-hunting.[26]

This process in turn provides greater justification for paying clerical workers low wages[27] in addition to creating boring routine jobs. What options are available? One woman put it this way: ". . . I do like my work. It's an interesting job. So each year . . . you say well, 'I'm unhappy with the salary.' Before you know it they say, 'Why don't you leave?' And you go to personnel and . . . you can look for what else there is on the bulletin board." Employers themselves seem to understand the clerks' desire to move up, and thus try to ameliorate the situation by upgrading the job without increasing wages. ". . . They change your job title from secretary to administrative assistant; no raise, big title. I told my boss right out, 'Keep the title. Give me the raise.'"

Sex-role steotyping of jobs also contributes to the dead-end quality of clerical work. The nature of the work, the lack of opportunity for mobility, the prevailing ideology about women's family roles type-cast women into the lowest-paid jobs with the least likelihood of promotion.[28] Attempts at mobility are frustrated at every step even among women who have opportunities for advancement. A woman working in a bank found these conditions:

> I believe banking is one of [the] commercial areas where women are very discriminated against. It is not an open or blatant discrimination, but rather for some reason the men are given, offered positions in areas of the banks where advancement is much more likely. Being unmarried, I have been openly asked whether I was dating anyone seriously (just in general conversation, of course!). I entered the bank in a management training program consisting of seven men and seven women. Now (22 months later) all of the men still at the bank have been placed in permanent positions and some in internal departments which are very prestigious, while there are still three girls yet to be given permanent positions.

The second subcategory involves the actual work itself. The deskilling process has increased the routinization and boring nature of the work and reduced the working knowledge of the clerk, and thus lessened her control over the work process.[29] Respondents were asked about job duties. There were a variety of job titles represented: legal secretary, key punch operator, administrative assistant, accounting clerk, among others. Duties included the full range of the expected — typing, filing, answering phones, record-keeping, dictation. Also included were the much-publicized personal work not specified in job descriptions that reflects the female status of the worker — getting coffee, listening to troubles, being a nursemaid. A few women found themselves in positions of responsibility, making decisions, running the office. But these jobs have their own sources of dissatisfaction, and for this reason it is in the interest of management to limit the office worker's responsibilities.

> [Secretaries] *do* know their bosses' jobs, and even do their bosses' work many times. But they're paid a "clerical" salary. This leads to problems of discontent and requests for raises. So it's better for the company if most people are uninformed and limited in understanding. This may make them more willing to accept their low pay gracefully, since their jobs aren't "worth" any more.[30]

When asked how they liked their work, most respondents were dissatisfied with the menial and boring nature of their jobs, describing themselves as being in a rut, and not having much responsibility. Some expressed the hope that they would not have to stay in these jobs. There is a high level of awareness of the negative effects of modern technology on their jobs. When asked about the use of word processors, one respondent replied, "I wouldn't want to be sitting in front of one of those things. I'm not a factory worker . . . I'd be better off going to Westinghouse or someplace like that, doing factory work, getting paid for factory work."

The menial nature of the work means more than boredom for these workers. Their dislike of it stems from their desire to have responsibility, to be able to be innovative with their work, to find work a challenge. An office administrator said, "It isn't really a rewarding position for me, plus the fact that there aren't many thank-yous makes it even worse. I'd like to get into something that's more creative and more challenging to me where the responsibility I take on is a challenge." A bank employee, who had reached the highest clerical position in her department stated, "You really can't be very innovative in your job. Everything has a tried and true pattern that you have to follow and you can't make any changes without going . . . to the manager. And you're not encouraged really to make any changes even if you thought of any." It is not only the lack of creativity built into the job but it's official discouragement when employees themselves find ways of improving the work process that leads to frustration. Only one woman expressed the opinion that lack of responsibility could have advantages. "In a way it's nice too, that your job tends to be nine to five. You know, you have no homework. You can leave it there, whereas if you had a more responsible position, you'd probably have to take work home or stay later." The assumption of this argument is that work and life are separate, an assumption that most of these women are fighting by involving themselves in an organization on their free time to improve working conditions.

Most of the respondents mentioned being asked to do domestic chores that were not specified in their job descriptions. They deeply resent this, and often refuse to do them. Making and getting coffee seems to be the most common of these chores. It has become a symbol of the division between management and the clerical staff, man and woman, in a system where paternalistic loyalty and traditional sex roles were once carried out without question. The modern office is in a transition state where it continues to be the advantage of the employer to try to exact loyalty and maintain the office as a substitute home, and the clerk as a substitute wife. Few of the rewards of the system remain for the clerk, and the issue of domestic chores becomes a focal point of dissatisfaction. One secretary describes her experience: "A directive came around, a memo, that women are supposed to take turns cleaning up the coffee room; go in there and clean it up and clean out the pot. And we all rebelled." Some of the resentment towards these expectations were based in the women's belief that if they were expected to do these menial tasks, then they weren't being taken seriously for doing the work for which they were hired:

> I want extra pay for making coffee. But I'm not a waitress. I said, "If you want a waitress, you can hire a waitress for a hell of a lot cheaper than you hired me . . . I don't get coffee. I don't run errands . . . I have enough of my own things to do on my own time. I'm here to work. That's all there is to it."

Thus, the working conditions of these clericals contributes to their dissatisfaction. The combination of low pay and little opportunity for promotion leads to real economic hardship as well as frustration with the lack of advancement to more rewarding work. The nature of the work itself generally requires less responsibility than the worker wishes to have, and becomes increasingly routine as computer technology takes over the office. At the same time, the domestic work requirements of many clericals are equally dissatisfying for other reasons based in traditional sex roles. In any case, the dissatisfaction of office workers is tied to their working conditions.

Work Relations

When discussing dissatisfaction with work, respondents often discuss the relationships they have with co-workers, supervisors, and employers. In general, the better those relationships, the less dissatisfaction they feel with their work. In fact, these relationships were considered by most to be a significant factor in what made their jobs bearable or unbearable as much as the work they did, their pay, or their chances for advancement. One key-punch operator who complained of low pay addressed this subject: "Why am I still working here? Because I like my work and the women in my department are nice."

Other women feel isolated on their jobs because they believe they are more discriminated against than their co-workers. One explained that this took the form of better wages and privileges that others had from which she was excluded. An older worker observed that older women in her office worked harder than their younger co-workers who tended to take long lunch hours, something she would not consider doing. She believed that her fear of her boss kept her working harder than younger women. Another woman observed a classic pattern of control used by employers — competition among co-workers:

> On the job a man will play a woman against a woman. Every now and then a man will say to me, "But I got you to do it because you do it so well." And I start to bristle with pride and suddenly I catch myself — Bastard — isn't that ridiculous, as if I'm that much better than anybody else.

The successful management of such competition plays on traditional work roles reinforced by traditional sex roles, leading to distrust among co-workers and cooptation by employers of potentially troublesome employees.

Threaded through this category is the question of respect. Baltimore Working Women, as well as its national affiliate use the issue of respect as a rallying point. Although it is never precisely defined, nearly everyone has examples of the lack of respect they have experienced as clericals. Low pay is seen as a sign of lack of respect. Talking about problems at work, one respondent had this to say:

> I think respect is the main one. If people would respect women's work, naturally your wages are going to go up. I think that's the problem with low wages. Women's work is looked down upon. It's not really considered important, and you're not going to be paid wages for something that's considered trivial.

The experience itself stems from the treatment they receive from others in superior positions, particularly their male bosses. Disrespectful treatment may take several forms. Some women described it in relation to lack of recognition, both of their work as well as their physical presence:

> There is little or no recognition of the importance of my job, until I'm sick or on vacation. Different people that I encounter [sic] day in and day out for years have never bother [sic] to introduce themselves or even to speak. This is especially true if you happen to be Black in my Department.

Repeatedly, the respondents in this study describe the perception of their jobs by others in such terms as "only a secretary" or "Joe's girl."

There is a general perception that the job requires few skills, and little intelligence. "They really don't have any concept of what I do, so they don't have the amount of respect for me of the other girls working in the office." One woman complained that she was

> . . . not given credit for have [sic] any intelligence at all . . . I found that I could not perform any tasks on my own that might require the use of my experience or my intelligence!! It's about time (they) place more value on . . . long-term clerical employees and give them the respect they deserve.

Again, doing domestic chores, such as making coffee, is raised as a significant issue, tied to respect. If work time is spent getting coffee, what then is the value of office work?

> I wouldn't like to feel that I had to make coffee everyday, and I had to clean the dishes . . . But if I felt like I had to do it and was looked at as a maid, that would be very offensive to me. And that a lot of times it's lack of respect for the job because they don't take office work seriously . . . 'cause they say, "Oh, you can get me my coffee," . . . but your job isn't that important. But if it's just a nicety and you have a real person who does respect you and do give respect as far as pay and nice working conditions, benefits and things like that — that's a form of respect. . . But just to have to do it as part of your job, or as secretary, is so menial . . . to be told you have to get the coffee, you have to clean it up . . . That's just not having respect for the job.

Lack of respect is also indicated by use of demeaning names. One woman working in a construction firm expresses her thoughts:

> . . . The one thing I hate, too, is being called a girl, and the people, especially in construction, since it's basically all men, they come, "Is the girl here?" Or people call you up on the telephone. They say, "Hello, honey." But I find this with men and women, and oh, God, I can't stand it, especially coming from a woman.

Clerical workers have to face not only the assumption that they are not intelligent, but being accused of it directly:

> . . . he started yelling at me because I couldn't understand something — like "Do you understand it?" I said, "No, I don't understand it. Could you explain it to me?" And then he started yelling. I said, "Well, I'm not hard of hearing. I just don't understand what you're saying." He said, "No, you're just dumb like all women. You need to be home washing dishes . . ."

When a supervisor is accused of this sort of attack, one woman reports, the accusation is cleverly turned around:

> He admits that he calls me dumb, but they dismiss it because they said he was joking. "Why are you so touchy today? Can't you take a little joke?"
>
> They accuse me of . . . not being professional when I don't want to say good morning or throw him kisses when he comes in after he's called me dumb or whatever the day before.

This combination of assumptions about clerical work and the women who perform it add up to treatment that women office workers see as demeaning. Nevertheless, the stereotype that the work does not require knowledge or is not important is contradicted by the experiences and ideas of those who do that work. While many complain that the work is often menial and uncreative, it is also seen as necessary to the successful functioning of the entire workplace. One legal secretary explains; "Secretarial work is very important. Everyone cannot be and is not cut out to be an executive . . . But no executive could be competent in his/her job without the efforts of his/her secretary. It's about time that fact was realized by management." An administrative aide expressed it this way:

> I find that clerical employees, who are almost always women, are treated as second class, menial workers by your so-called "professionals." Isn't it a shame they can't be made aware of the fact that without us the office would not function; and even though were [sic] are in clerical positions, some of your brightest people can be found in these positions.

A number of respondents reported experiences of intimidation by supervisors or employers. This took three forms. The first was related to work expectations. Several women described how supervisors keep close watch over their work and the time spent away from work (lunch breaks, going to the bathroom), which is based on distrust of the worker. Often, workers find ways of getting around this form of intimidation through the use of sabotage.

Another form of intimidation is sexual harassment, one of the most highly publicized aspects of office work. Sexual harassment is another example of how ideology is reflected in work roles. The idea of women as sexual fair game gets played out daily in the workplace. For the most part men do not have any fear of reprisal, although there are now some legal avenues women can pursue if they have been sexually harassed. Experiences of this sort range from verbal comments to physical contact. Often statements are made with just enough innuendo as to make it difficult to accuse someone of harassment. ". . . Every man feels it is his right to constantly make suggestive remarks, sexual references or even to touch and hug in a way that can be interpreted innocently. Women who try to tolerate this are abused, those who reject it are considered snobby." None of the women were pleased with this sort of attention. They all saw it as negative, but there were a variety of responses, ranging from trying to ignore it, to pretending to take it as a compliment, to outright verbal complaints and threats of reporting the incidents. Most agree that these responses only put off the harassment for short periods of time, and that there is little advantage for the woman office worker regardless of her response. One woman expressed it this way:

> If he doesn't say "you're fired," and he just out and out harasses me every now and then, I just say to him, "I'd like to thank you for all the attention that you're paying me." I give him some of the same attention back. Then I go home and shed my little tears. Then I come back to work holding my head up in the air and say, "I wonder what type of harassment he's going to give me today?" But I feel like this: when he's harassing me and if I decide to quit, and I'm out there on the employment line, he's the one that's smiling because he still has his income to pay his bills, where I don't. So, I take . . . harassment as a form of a compliment because he's paying so much attention to me. And I try to tell a lot of people—do that and you'll find yourself with a lot more peace of mind, even though he may throw you in a little closet, with no telephone, with paper piled higher than your head. Just say, okay, if this is where I have to work, I know in an hour's time I'll go on a 15 minute break. I know that in two hours' time I'll be ready to go to lunch. At least I'll have a breather, but during that time, I'm still holding my head up, smiling, and I just let it go at that.

Other women are not so likely to passively accept sexual harassment and have had their jobs threatened as a result. One such office worker has had repeated problems with her boss, whose behavior, she reported, improved only after her complaints and threats to call his wife. Harassment does not only apply to behavior on the job. One secretary described her experience of being fired because the man she was dating, who was very influential in her boss's profession, disliked the idea of her dating other men. A more common experience is in companies whose policy demands that employers not fraternize outside the workplace. When such activities are discovered between male professionals and female secretaries, punishment is invariably harsher for the woman involved.

The third type of intimidation reported by respondents results either from efforts on the part of women to improve their jobs as individuals, to organize the workplace, or simply from the awareness that they are part of a working women's organization. Overall, the attitude on the part of employers is that the person who has complained about job conditions is simply a misfit. One woman concerned about false job descriptions and lack of training said, "When I complained . . . their response was that I was not adjusting well."

Apparently employers find that their employee's membership in Baltimore Working Women is quite threatening and a number of women have reported being intimidated for their interest or participation in this group. Several women were told they would be fired if they filled out surveys distributed by BWW and others believed that, if it were known they were members, this would happen. The women themselves are often surprised by the intensity of their bosses' fears:

> Every now and then they really flatter me. When the office manager comes to me and shakes his finger at me and says, "If you bring the union in here we will have to fire you." I feel very flattered. I really think maybe I'm more of a threat than I think.

The intimidation experienced by these office workers puts increased stress on their relations with people in the office as well as threatens the security of their jobs. Even those who do not fear being fired express the desire to leave jobs due to intimidation, yet often find themselves waiting a long time for a better opportunity to present itself. The knowledge that other situations might offer the same type of intimidation does not inspire women to look for other work.

We should not be surprised that clerical workers are dissatisfied with their jobs. The combination of the objective structural conditions and the workers' expectations of a decent work experience lead inevitably to discontent. What is done with this discontent? If it remains a generalized frustration in the lives of individual women, then it goes no further than individual attempts to understand or correct the problem. But, in fact, we see organizations spreading all over the country that address this discontent. The link between dissatisfaction and collective action is the growth of consciousness about one's social situation. The next chapter examines the types of consciousness that have developed among those women who seek collective solutions to job dissatisfaction.

NOTES

1. Jean Tepperman, *Not Servants, Not Machines: Office Workers Speak Out* (Boston: Beacon Press, 1976), p. 44.

2. Gabriel Kolko, "Working Wives: Their Effects on the Structure of the Working Class," *Science and Society* 42 (1978):261–63.

3. Ibid., p. 263.

4. Sally Hillsman Baker, "Women in Blue-Collar and Service Occupations," in Ann H. Stromberg and Shirley Harkess (eds.) *Women Working: Theories and Facts in Perspective* (Palo Alto, California: Mayfield, 1978), p. 343.

5. Kolko, "Working Wives," p. 271.

6. Ibid., p. 273; Mary Kathleen Benet, *Secretary: Enquiry into the Female Ghetto* (London: Sedgwick and Jackson, 1972), p. 150.

7. Kolko, "Working Wives," pp. 261–62; Francine D. Blau, "The Data on Women Workers, Past, Present, and Future," in Ann Stromberg and Shirley Harkess (eds.) *Women Working: Theories and Facts in Perspective.* (Palo Alto, California: Mayfield, 1978) pp. 38–39.

8. Marilyn Power Goldberg, "The Economic Exploitation of Women," in Richard C. Edwards, Michael Reich, and Thomas E. Weisskopf (eds.) *The Capitalist System: A Radical Analysis of American Society* (Englewood Cliffs, N.J.: Prentice-Hall, 1972), p. 342.

9. Benet, *Secretary: Enquiry into the Female Ghetto*, p. 150.

10. Virginia L. Olesen and Frances Katsuranis, "Urban Nomads: Women in Temporary Clerical Services," in *Women Working: Theories and Facts in Perspective*, ed. Ann H. Stromberg and Shirley Harkess (Palo Alto, California: Mayfield, 1978), p. 319. See also Rosabeth Moss Kanter, "Women and the Structure of Organizations: Explorations in Theory and Behavior," in Marcia Millman and Rosabeth Moss Kanter (eds.) *Another Voice: Feminist Perspectives on Social Life and Social Sciences* (New York: Anchor Books, 1975), pp. 54–55.

11. Olesen and Katsuranis, "Urban Nomads," pp. 330–32.

12. Goldberg, "The Economic Exploitation of Women," pp. 343–44.

13. Olesen and Katsuranis, "Urban Nomads," p. 334.

14. David Lockwood, *The Blackcoated Worker: A Study in Class Consciousness* (London: Ruskin House, George Allen and Unwin, Ltd., 1958), p. 99; Benet, *Secretary: Enquiry into the Female Ghetto*, pp. 40–41.

15. Lockwood, *The Blackcoated Worker*, pp. 125–26.

16. Ibid., pp. 124–25.

17. Tepperman, *Not Servants; Not Machines*, p. 55.

18. Harry Braverman, *Labor Monopoly Capital: The Degradation of Work in the Twentieth Century* (New York: Monthly Review Press, 1974), pp. 315–16; Everett M. Kassalow, "White-Collar Unionism in The United States," in *White-Collar Trade Unions. Contemporary Developments in Industrialized Societies*, ed. Adolf Sturmthal (Chicago: University of Illinois Press, 1967), p. 358; Benet, *Secretary: Enquiry into the Female Ghetto*, pp. 146–47; Evelyn Nakano Glenn and Roslyn L. Feldberg, "Clerical Work: The Female Occupation," in *Women: A Feminist Perspective*, 2nd edition, ed. Jo Freeman (Palo Alto, California: Mayfield, 1979), pp. 324–25.

19. Tepperman, *Not Servants, Not Machines*, pp. 41–42.

20. Glenn and Feldberg, "Clerical Work: The Female Occupation," p. 315.

21. Tepperman, *Not Servants, Not Machines*, p. 57.

22. Tepperman, *Not Servants, Not Machines*, p. 41; see also Glenn and Feldberg, "Clerical Work: The Female Occupation," p. 324.

23. Job satisfaction among clerical workers has been studied previously. Among those most pertinent to this research are: Benet, *Secretary: Enquiry into the Female Ghetto*; Michel Crozier, *The World of the Office Worker* (Chicago: The University of Chicago Press, 1971); Albert A. Blum, Martin Estey, James W. Kuhn, Wesley A. Wildman, and Leo Troy, *White-Collar Workers* (New York: Random House, 1971).

24. Lockwood, *The Blackcoated Worker*, p. 62.

25. Braverman, *Labor and Monopoly Capital*, pp. 315–26; Glenn and Feldberg, "Clerical Work: The Female Occupation," pp. 324–25; Benet, *Secretary: Enquiry into the*

Female Ghetto, pp. 145–46; Kassalow, "White Collar Unionism," pp. 357–58.

26. Tepperman, *Not Servants, Not Machines*, pp. 42–43.

27. Louise Kapp Howe, *Pink Collar Workers: Inside the World of Women's Work* (New York: Avon, 1978), p. 57.

28. Kanter, "Women and the Structure of Organizations," p. 51.

29. Braverman, *Labor and Monopoly Capital*, pp. 335–39; for a thorough discussion of working knowledge, see Ken C. Kusterer, *Know-How on the Job: The Important Working Knowledge of "Unskilled" Workers.* (Boulder, Colorado: Westview Press, 1978.)

30. Tepperman, *Not Servants, Not Machines*, p. 59.

Chapter 5

The Character of Consciousness among Women Office Workers

INTRODUCTION

There is general agreement today that clerical workers share the same social class as manual workers if one uses a Marxian analysis of class based on property ownership and control.[1] The growing similarities in workplace structure and working conditions also contribute to this evaluation. If one is interested in understanding the experiences of clerical workers that may lead to class consciousness, a whole realm of subjective factors specific to the clerical sector come into play. Some of these overlap the experiences of manual workers, but many do not, and the consciousness of office workers as members of the working class must be understood in the context of the office, its structure, and the nature of control that takes place there. Social relations among workers and between workers and bosses is also a critical area of experience. Therefore, while we understand that office workers are part of the working class, we must be careful not to assume that differences do not exist among various sectors within the working class.

> . . . such a broad definition of class has the disadvantage of obscuring actual variations in the situation and experience of those who share the common position of "propertyless" labour. It is quite obvious that Marx himself clearly realized that the mere fact of "propertylessness" provided no explanation of the actual presence or absence of class consciousness in a group. What he regarded as decisive for the development of class consciousness were the actual experiences to which the members of a class were subjected by reason of their common economic position. And by this he understood not only the material deprivations or indulgences which they shared, but also the sense of alienation from other classes and

the sense of identification with one another which they experienced in
the social relationships of production.[2]

Furthermore, if we want to grasp the consciousness of women clerical
workers, additional significant factors come into play. The ideology of
patriarchy, the practice of sexism and, very central to this, women's daily
experience of balancing responsibilities in the home and the office are
crucial factors in the development of a particular kind of consciousness.
External influences such as the presence of the women's movement also
have significant impact. To sort out these factors and give them meaning
in the concrete experiences of women clerical workers who are activists in
Baltimore Working Women is the purpose of this chapter.

The response of women office workers to their job experiences, opportunities to organize, family responsibilities, and awareness of sexism in
the workplace and in other areas, as it applies to the female clerk, lead to
a unique consciousness that reflects those very experiences from which it is
derived. There are three main sources of this consciousness: the workplace, women's expected sex roles, and social-class position. These sources
are represented in three types of consciousness examined in this chapter:
job consciousness, feminist consciousness, and class consciousness. Each
will be discussed in terms of its contribution to the overall development of
consciousness among these women, and will be tied to the development of
activism in a working women's organization.

HOW THE STRUCTURE OF THE OFFICE
CONTRIBUTES TO THE DEVELOPMENT
OF CONSCIOUSNESS

In addition to the basic contradictions experienced by women between the home and the workplace, there are factors specific to office
work that magnify those contradictions. In *Contested Terrain*, Richard
Edwards argues that control over the workplace is a critical factor in the
relationships between management and labor, and that different segments of the labor market are subject to different types of control. During
the nineteenth century, with businesses being relatively small and technologically unsophisticated, simple control based on the personal power
of the capitalist sufficed in most situations. But with the twentieth century we see both increased size of the workplace and growing complexity
of machinery, causing the need for the forms of control to change.

Large firms developed methods of organization that are more formalized and more consciously contrived than simple control; they are

"structural" forms of control. Two possibilities existed: more formal, consciously contrived controls could be embedded in either the physical structure of the labor process (producing "technical" control) or in its social structure (producing "bureaucratic" control). In time, employers used both, for they found that the new systems made control more institutional and hence less visible to workers, and they also provided a means for capitalists to control the "intermediate layers," those extended lines of supervision and power.[3]

Edwards goes on to point out that all three types of control persist and that specific segments of the labor market are subject to each type of control. He divides this labor market into the following three segments. The first is the *secondary market*, including primarily low-skilled service, retail, clerical and migrant agricultural workers, characterized by low wages, high insecurity, little opportunity for advancement. The second segment contains the *subordinate primary market* in which we find both blue-collar and white-collar workers, whose jobs are generally routine, needing limited skills or training. These jobs are often unionized and rewarded with good wages and a seniority system. Third, there is the *independent primary market* made up of jobs requiring specialized skills and education. These are generally professional jobs characterized by a fair amount of independence, high wages, and opportunities for promotion. We find a variety of crafts represented such as plumbers and electricians as well as professionals like doctors, lawyers, and scientists.[4]

The importance of delineating these labor market segments here is found in the different types of control that predominate in each:

Labor markets are segmented because they express a historical segmentation of the labor process; specifically, a distinct system of control inside the firm underlies each of the three market segments. The secondary labor market is the market expression of workplaces organized according to simple control. The subordinate primary market contains those workplaces (workers and jobs) under the "mixed" system of technical control and unions. And the independent primary market reflects bureaucratically controlled labor processes. Thus, the fundamental basis for division into three segments is to be found in the workplace, not in the labor market; so to define the three market segments we now have a single criterion — the type of control system — rather than simply a cluster of market behavior characteristics.[5]

Given the different job experiences based not only on the nature of the work, but more significantly on the type of control used over the workforce, workers in different segments exhibit different responses to control. Further, the historical transition from one type of control to another, and the mix of types of control in many worksettings adds to the complexity of the relationship between workers and their employers as well as workers in one segment to workers in another, and clearly must affect the potential for class consciousness.

Using Edwards' typology, the placing of the clerical workforce in a particular segment is a difficult task. It is clear that clerical work is found in both the secondary and subordinate primary markets, depending on the specific job being examined. Clerical jobs fall into the secondary market, using Edwards' definition given their experiences with low pay, few promotion opportunities, lack of security, and absence of unionization. But there is a significant minority, particularly among the respondents in this study, that falls within the subordinate primary market, fitting most of the characteristics except unionization. Further, the nature of clerical work with its particular historical relationship between employer and worker, and the relatively slow development of office technology until quite recently, caused it to remain in the realm of simple control much longer than most jobs in those labor market segments. Until the recent development of sophisticated office machinery it was virtually impossible to routinize or objectively evaluate office work as has been done in factories since the advent of modern industrialization. Consequently, clerical work did not lend itself to technical control until recently, relying instead on the personal judgment of those in power, as is characteristic of simple control. That the clerical workforce is primarily women while their supervisors are men contributed to the maintenance of a system of control that was ideologically acceptable in the context of the patriarchal nature of that work setting. The domestic patterns of work and relationships in the traditional office, where workers and bosses carried out traditional sex roles served the personal power of the bosses necessary under a system of simple control. Thus it is in the interest of employers to maintain patriarchal power in the office. This is carried out in part by maintaining sex-segregated jobs. Simple control prevents women from identifying with other workers on a large scale by keeping the relationships between workers and bosses personal and job descriptions vague.

In her classic study of women who work for the telephone company, Elinor Langer observed that the consciousness of the workers was limited in this way:

> The women do not see themselves as "workers" in anything like the classical sense. The absence of this consciousness — deliberately stunted by management personnel strategies — is a natural and realistic response to the conditions of their work. Customer's Service Representative is the position from which lower (female) management is recruited, and promotions are frequent. Supervisors are always former Representatives and their relations with the women they supervise are close and friendly.

> The absence of rigid job definitions is an economic boon to the company as well as a psychic advantage to the employees.[6]

It is not just the internal dynamics of the office that are served by the use of simple control. Capitalism as a whole has benefitted. Since the early twentieth century, the demands of capitalist development have made it necessary to include women as a permanent source of labor. It is able to maintain control over this sector of workers partially through traditional sex role expectations that continue to define women first as wives and mothers and only secondarily as wage-earning workers.

> The use of the labour of married women in advanced capitalism is part of complicated changes in the structure and organization of work, as well as the need always to find new markets and to effect continual changes in the nature of demand. Despite the dependence of capitalism now on married women as a permanent and essential part of the work force, employers are still apt to behave as if they were doing women a favor by employing them. They still act as if women should somehow be grateful for the chance to be exploited. This is particularly ironic in view of the actual nature of the jobs which are categorized as "women's work." The only factor these jobs really have in common is low pay, which means the profit capitalism takes from women is direct and crude. The cheap labour of women is an alternative to investing in machinery.[7]

The evidence presented in this study shows that members of a working women's organization no longer buy into that ideology, if they ever really did, and as has already been shown many are aware of the relationship between the low pay of women workers and company profits.

Few offices are structured today in a way in which simple control alone can be effective. Other forms of control also operate. Yet the ideology that served simple control persists and is often successfully acted out. The contradictions inherent in trying to use simple control in a setting in which it is no longer structurally appropriate are manifest in such issues as sexual harassment, demands for job descriptions, objective evaluations of work, and that seemingly amorphous issue of respect. Nevertheless, the necessity of calling for action on these issues implies that, at least to some extent, simple control is still being used successfully. Within this context, both technical control and bureaucratic control have emerged as more effective overall in controlling office workers.

The role of technical control is the most direct and easy to examine in terms of its effect on clerical work. Large companies in particular have taken advantage of new office technology, reorganizing their offices to fit the technical requirements of word processors and other computers that regulate the work pace, the personal style of the worker, and standardize the work process, the effects being a deskilled, technically controlled workforce.[8] Technical control has long been the primary source of control by employers in industry, with the workforce responding by efforts of control on their part through unions. It is not suprising that office workers also respond to this type of control by collective organizing in working women's organizations, and increasingly, with unionization. Technical control offers a clearcut view of the relationship between management and worker as an adversary one and not subject to personal or individual evaluation. Thus, it is not difficult to understand the growth of class consciousness and collective efforts to resist this form of control.

Bureaucratic control is somewhat more complex as it affects the office structure through institutional rules and regulations, strictly defined job descriptions and requirements, and hierarchical patterns of power. There is no machine setting the pace or defining the limits of creativity, but rather a new set of relationships among workers in various strata in an organization. Bureaucratic control almost universally applies to management and professional staff, and by virtue of its existence at that level must influence lower levels such as the clerical staff. But it is also used indirectly to control clerical workers along with simple control and technical control. One important effect of bureaucratic control is the increased stratification of the office. Running a bureaucracy requires compartmentalizing jobs and regulating them hierarchically. As a result we find that ". . . *social* or *organizational* distinctions (always supplemented, of course, by differences both in power and in technical function) become the basis for ranking and advancement."[9] Within each labor market segment found in the office, there are structured ways in which to be evaluated and move up. But to move from the secondary market or subordinate primary market where clerical workers are found, into the independent primary market is quite difficult. It can be done occasionally, and is based on behaving in a way so as to contribute to increased bureaucratic control rather than fulfilling actual work assignments successfully.

> Workers who consistently behave properly (that is, in accord with the established criteria) are valuable to the corporation. Such workers have attributes much akin to technical skill. Just as technical skills make possible the operation of the firm's physical technology, so these behavior traits facilitate the firm's control. Employers seek out and reward workers with the right behavior traits.[10]

Yet the opportunity for the office clerk to do this is limited by the other forms of control imposed upon her. The personal power of the boss characteristic of simple control may overlook her ability to follow rules, and the woman is judged instead by her personal loyalty, sexual attractiveness, or pleasant personality. Technical control also serves to limit her chances to show her ability to behave according to bureaucratic rules when her work life is dominated by the routinization of machinery. Even more directly, the nature of clerical work can facilitate bureaucratic control since the office worker is valued primarily for her ability to complete tasks (technical control) and present herself in a way acceptable to a patriarchally defined work environment (simple control). As indicated in the earlier discussion on work dissatisfaction, a number of respondents in this study expressed frustration at their inability to advance at their jobs beyond the highest level allowed for the clerical staff. Often they move up quickly from low-level to high-level clerical work or from secondary to subordinate primary positions, but at that point the job becomes dead end. They are aware that few people in the secretarial field move into management in part because further education or specific training is required, yet it is not offered to the clerical staff. Employers make it a point to discourage movement of this sort. In one case, a respondent reported that her boss told her that she had set goals for herself that were too high:

> I feel as though my goals are not that high, and it's just the point of reaching those goals which I thought by age thirty I could at least have reached my goals as far as the secretarial field, and then eventually branch out into managerial type of work. But so far, that has not happened, and for that reason I feel stagnated. And it's frustrating at times knowing that you can do things and improve yourself but you don't have the opportunity to do it.

We see, then, that the clerical worker is subject to three different types of control that make different, even contradictory demands upon her. First, she must respond to the power of her employer by being acceptable to his personal definition of a good office worker. Second, she must adjust her work patterns to the new technologies being brought into the office. Third, she must conform to the office structure defined by bureaucratic regulations to which the managerial and professional staff are tied.

It may appear that control is then complete, but instead we find contradictions among types of control that may promote discontent among office workers. For instance, sexual harassment, which might be common under a system of simple control, has no place in a bureaucratically controlled system. Thus secretaries begin to resist it when they are provided with a form of control that excludes it. The issue of respect with which office workers are so concerned makes sense in the context of the three sources of control. Lack of respect can come from the expression of personal power of bosses under the form of simple control, or it may stem from the factory-like conditions created through technical control, in which those whose work life is controlled by machines are categorically not respected. But bureaucratic control does not judge respect in this way. If you play your role properly, you are an accepted participant in the company. Proper behavior, adhering to rules, regardless of your job, generates respect. This is not to say that individuals do not vary in regard to the amount of respect they generate, but this is due to their ability to carry out their work, not what that work is. Respondents repeatedly say that clerical work is not respected, goes unnoticed, and because of that, they as individuals are not respected. Secondary and subordinate primary market jobs carry with them simple and technical types of control and the issue of respect is very much intertwined with those forms of control. In the independent primary market, under bureaucratic control, respect is assumed.

It is clear that bureaucratic control on the whole is more advantageous than simple control in large companies, since control is built into the social structure. Yet, because of the unique position of clerks, their status as females, their availability on the market, and the role of technical control in those places where use of machinery is widespread, bureaucratic control is applied in a limited and inconsistent fashion. For example, use of job descriptions is characteristic in a system of bureaucratic control. Yet so few office workers have them that they have become a major issue for working women's organizations. We see situations in which clerical workers are demanding job descriptions, and large companies (in the case of Baltimore, a large bank), are resisting establishing them for the clerical staff. Clearly, they are seen as a disadvantage to those companies who believe other forms of control are adequate for their office staff. The workers, on the other hand, see lack of job descriptions as a way to perpetuate or increase their exploitation, by getting them to perform tasks that would never be written into a job description. These tasks often fall into the domestic realm, such as making coffee, watering plants, cleaning the office, and running personal errands for the boss; those very tasks that are acceptable under the system of simple control and that are often focal points of discontent among office workers. This scenario is encouraged, once again, by the patriarchal structure of the workplace, men being bosses and women being helpmates, and assumptions about traditional sex roles that carry over from the family. On the other hand, the rapid increase of sophisticated office machinery creates a situation in which women clerical workers find themselves working without a supervisor present, or where they must work for several men, making it difficult to carry out any of the relationships common in a system of simple control.

Further, with increased technology, her skills are limited and thus her job security and potential for advancement become severely curtailed. Because of the recent influx of such technology into offices, many women as well as their employers have had to make rapid adjustments to a new form of technical control, with both simple control and bureaucratic control lurking in the background. Office workers at different hierarchical levels in the same company must adhere to different types of control, depending upon whether they are private secretaries, working in the typing pool, or operating a computer. This arrangement is confusing at best. One important effect is that it acts to cloud the differences between "them and us," classic distinctions made freely in industrial work between workers and management.[11] This in itself makes it more difficult for office workers to get a sense of class identity with other workers at different levels in the hierarchy or in production work. On the other hand, it presents office workers with glaring differences in types of control from which they can observe potential improvements in their own working conditions. The more bureaucratized office structure gets, the less clerical workers will put up with simple control. None of these types of control gives ultimate power to the worker to be sure, but bureaucratic control is certainly more liberalizing, as it does not depend on the whim of an autocratic boss. It is a sophisticated type of control, and more appropriate to the modern office, yet it is still to the advantage of management to maintain personal control at the lowest levels of the clerical staff when possible. This can only be understood as an extension of patriarchy. Examples of patriarchal power remain even at the highest levels of the corporate world—women executives, too, experience sexism—but are especially rampant in the relationships between male boss and female secretary. Bureaucratizing control in this situation frees the secretary from patriarchal control in much the same way the historical rise of capitalism freed women from the slavery of the precapitalist patriarchal family.

Being judged on the basis of bureaucratic regulations is a form of control to be sure, but it is restrictive in quite a different way from that of simple control. The worker is expected to be loyal to the company in return for job security.[12] It involves not simply getting tasks done, but contributing to the overall effectiveness of the bureaucratic system that gets rewarded. One is promoted if one behaves effectively in this manner.[13] Despite the effectiveness of this type of control, it has its own set of contradictions opening the way to further change.

> . . . job security and a long-lasting identification with the company also provide precisely those conditions that are most likely to foster demands among workers for more say in establishing the rules by which the enter-

prise is run. Secure workers expecting to stay with their corporate
employers over long periods turn to issues of quality and control of
work. Thus, in establishing those conditions most favorable for bureaucratic control, capitalists inadvertently have also established the conditions under which demands for workplace democracy flourish. Such
demands constitute a potentially fundamental challenge to employers'
power.[14]

Many of the most active respondents in this study are long-term,
well-paid, upper-level clericals, who work within the framework of
bureaucratic control. Their satisfaction with their own working conditions does not stop them from questioning that control and has led them to
an organization that calls for rights for office workers. The above remarks
help explain their position from the standpoint of how the structure of
control in the workplace gives rise to the potential for significant altera-
tion of power therein. This awareness of a need for change is not revolutionary. At this stage, from the evidence found in this research,
respondents report that they are most interested in working under conditions similar to managers and professionals in terms of security, pay, promotions, and job descriptions. They are opting for bureaucratic control as
an improvement upon simple and technical forms of control. From the
data gathered in this study, only a very few respondents saw the potential
for more radical changes that are theoretically inherent in bureaucratic
control, thus limiting the degree to which class consciousness develops.

We can see that the structure of the office with the influence of
several types of control offers the clerical worker a confusing conception
of power. While these forms of power may at times reinforce one another,
they may also be contradictory in their manifestations. Many of the issues
that clerical workers raise as points of dissatisfaction derive from those
contradictions. The examples given above, sexual harassment, respect,
job descriptions, and limited advancement are coupled with problems
found in the work itself, its routinization, and in the low pay, to create a
particular kind of consciousness. This consciousness can be seen as limited
by the particular position of office workers, yet that very position offers
clerical workers a unique view of class differences. That view is undoubtedly confusing, given the hierarchy in the office that creates artificial
divisions among workers, the use of technology that is alienating, and the
use of personal patriarchal power to control the clerk. But it may be that
this confusion itself gives rise to dissatisfactions, which may then contribute to consciousness and militant activism.

Using this understanding of the types of control in the office as a
structural foundation, we can now address the development of consciousness among women office workers, as revealed by the respondents in this
study.

JOB CONSCIOUSNESS

Job consciousness is represented by the respondent's opinions and attitudes about clerical work and the working conditions that would lead office workers to being dissatisfied, as described in Chapter 4. These problems were either experienced firsthand by the respondents, or were reported as a general condition of office work. In either case, respondents were well aware that such experiences were not isolated. Thus, nearly everyone interviewed could be considered to have job consciousness, an awareness of shared problems in a specific job setting.

Job consciousness is manifest in several ways. The most relevant here is by becoming a member of a working women's organization and participating in its various activities. It is not the activism itself that indicates consciousness, but rather how the participant views her experience in the organization. Why people join the organization has been discussed previously, but a short summary here would be useful. Gaining knowledge about one's rights as a working woman and a desire to help other working women topped the list in the survey that was conducted. Another popular response was to improve overall working conditions. When interviewed, respondents commonly expressed these themes as well as concern about specific problems at their particular places of employment. These responses can be understood in the context of job consciousness by applying more generalizable categories to those described above. Most responses fall into one of two categories: practicability and solidarity.

Practicability

Practicability refers to specific gaining of information to help people deal with job problems and increase general knowledge. It is carried out in the form of workshops, presentations, and written information sheets. While it has the obvious purpose of helping individuals cope with their own job problems, it also inevitably points out that these problems are shared. A woman who attends meetings to gain this knowledge cannot help but recognize that she is not the only one with these problems. This is the first step to raising job consciousness, and many members who originally came to meetings for this reason have increased job consciousness. The next step, then, is solidarity with others.

Solidarity

Here we are speaking of an identification with others in the same predicament. People tend to join the organization because they already feel a sense of solidarity once they become involved. Thus, job consciousness is a motivator for joining the group as well as something that increases as one's participation increases. Respondents often describe their appreciation of the solidarity found in the group, noting that they feel isolated at work, and that "there is strength in numbers." Those who recognize that co-workers share their problems but are unwilling to act on them find the organization useful:

> A lot of girls at work, they're going through the same thing that I am, but it's like out of fear for the job . . . They grouch about it and then it blows over and they work a little while longer until it comes up again. So I feel that at least I'm making an effort to try to change, with other women, to try to change what I don't like.

We see here a recognition of shared job conditions and a need to improve them through collective effort.

Regularly being made aware that others share the same job conditions is an important motivator for members. It not only contributes to job consciousness, but also increases the activism of the members:

> I'm always up after a meeting. I always have a good, positive feeling from it. I feel challenged by it. I mean, I can go to a meeting and hear a story about somebody who got passed over for a promotion or somebody who was fighting for a job description and couldn't get it or this or that, and it just feeds my fire a little bit more. It gets me a little bit more up and psyched to get things accomplished . . . It's not the type of thing where I come home discouraged that it's still going on. I see the headway we're starting to make, and feel very positive about it. It gives me a really good feeling to know that I'm part of it.

One of the most significant findings of this research is that many members presently have satisfactory job situations, yet feel the need to help others out of a sense of solidarity. These are people whose job consciousness was high before they became members. Many of these women had previously worked under unsatisfactory conditions and managed to individually improve their jobs. Nevertheless, they saw those conditions as structurally based and chose to help others. A staff member describes it this way:

> I think the first women who got involved tended to be women who had job problems and who had dealt with them and who felt a sense of either anger or bitterness or just awareness that a lot of women had about the same kind of problems, and didn't know what to do . . .

Testimony from members verifies her observation. One woman who said that belonging to the organization has made her less self-centered and more of a "team person" explains it this way: "I'm very happy where I am workwise and moneywise, but I know there are people out there working for $125 a week and I just feel so sorry for them. I'd like to do something to help them." Another very active member who had extricated herself from a typically bad job at a bank explains; "I became involved with the banking committee because of the many friends I left behind that worked at _____ Bank and because I feel a personal commitment to try to help those I left behind." Still another active member describes her altruism in more general terms. Membership in the organization has increased her awareness and activism. "I feel I'm more committed to things that I feel are right. I feel that women really get the shaft at work and all, and I can see concrete ways to improve it."

Solidarity is also expressed on the job, and often takes the form of sharing information with others and acting together to increase workers' power. Some respondents describe this as sabotage. Just as making coffee has been a symbol of "women's place" in the office, it is seen as a weapon by secretaries. One member describes how it is used in her office:

> . . . that's one thing we discuss all the time. And we told people different ways they can get out of it. Y'know, you throw salt in the coffee so that it tastes so awful they never ask you to make it again. You use three packs of coffee to make it. Y'know, play dumb and they will never ask you to touch it again.

Another describes her position as a secretary who opens mail as an opportunity to gather information about the company that can later be used to her advantage. Still another described several ways in which employees in her company acted together against their bosses. In this case, computer operators patched up windows to make it difficult for supervisors to observe them working. Furthermore, through discussion and experimentation, they learned how to jam the computers so that they had to shut down for short periods of time. Why was this done? "For a lot of reasons. Number one was that they were demoting us. And they didn't tell us. Everybody in the company knew but us. So when we found out we just sabotaged them." This same woman claims that this is a common practice: "I found that everywhere I worked somebody knew how to mess them up."

The awareness of the importance of office work among those who do that work is often discussed. Clerical workers realize that many employers do not recognize the importance of office work, and imagine ways to correct that. One woman who genuinely likes her job, and has no wish to move into a supervisory position, regrets the lack of recognition for the difficulty of her job and the amount of responsibility she takes on. "I work a job that only two of us do. If both of us decided to call in sick one day, they'd be in trouble." Others express this notion on a grander scale. Two similar fantasies: "I want to see on National Secretaries' Day . . . everybody wave through the windows to each other, or walk down the street for five minutes and just see the power that they have." And:

> The point has been made jokingly that if we could get everybody in downtown Baltimore that worked in offices to just walk out for one hour, that all of downtown would shut down. That's how important I think that the jobs are that we're doing. I just wish that we could carry that out.

What more concrete evidence of job consciousness is there than a desire for outward manifestations of solidarity of this sort? Yet, job consciousness in itself does not necessarily lead to worker organizations or militancy, or even to individual actions such as confrontations with supervisors or sabotage. Such actions are often oriented to solving specific problems like pay, or some aspect of worker control. Generally speaking, even these issues are often seen as separate from one another and not as part of a larger structural relationship between employer and employee based on capitalist relations of production.[15] Thus, action is limited by the degree of consciousness. Theoretically, responses of workers at this level may be seen as inherently conservative, or at best, reformist when consciousness and action are never taken beyond the specifics of workplace issues. This arrangement assumes that if one sees problems as stemming only from the particular situation of a specific type of work, in this case, clerical, then solutions to problems also apply only to that situation. For most workers job dissatisfaction is not consciously tied to the economic structure as a whole.

> Workers are still oriented toward making demands on companies and unions, and do not aim at taking autonomous control over their own lives. Within the American working class, no significant movement or section of workers defines itself as a class and sees its mission to be the same as the liberation of society from corporate capitalist social relations.[16]

Clearly, the women in this movement see the need to organize, that employees need not (and should not) face these problems alone. Respondents consistently supported the notion of collective organizing and activism as the best approach to solving the major problems women office workers face. Yet the question remains, does such an organization address itself only to job-related issues, accepting the basic premise that it is the employer's right to own and control production? If consciousness remains on the level of "job consciousness," activities in the organization will be limited in their scope to solving specific job-related problems, accepting the structure of the capitalist-based workplace. Yet, the very structure of this organization lends itself to a broader analysis, given its widespread city-based membership of people in a variety of workplaces and jobs, and on a national level, even greater diversity. Thus, while each action in itself may address particular establishments and issues, those actions are selected that address the broadest possible set of conditions experienced by women office workers in that city, rather than attempting to organize workers at one particular job site over issues specific to that place of employment. Thus the potential for developing beyond job consciousness is enhanced for the membership. Furthermore, the experiences of women as workers contributes to an awareness complementary to job consciousness and containing a second dimension that compounds the understanding members have of their situation. This second dimension is called feminist consciousness.

FEMINIST CONSCIOUSNESS

Feminist consciousness is represented by an awareness of problems specific to women both in and outside the workplace, especially in the family. Experiences tied to women's inferior social status are seen as based in the ideology and practice of sexism.

When asked why they thought women experienced problems at work, a range of responses were expressed which represent the ideology of sexism. A few respondents described the problem in historical terms: "I guess they feel that we're not intelligent. It's tradition. It's always been that way, and even though people may not consciously think that way, it's ingrained there. They're not used to thinking any differently." and: "We're always one step behind the man, sometimes even more steps than one step behind the man, and it's given women the attitude over hundreds and hundreds of years that we're of lesser importance to the rest of the world simply because we're women." These women see ideology as having an historical base and that it affects the attitudes of both men and women towards the place of women in society. Yet these opinions only vaguely suggest the structural conditions that manifest themselves in oppressive circumstances for women today.

Most respondents believe the sources of sexism are to be found in an ideology of male supremacy that protects the power men have over women:

> I think we're a threat to a lot of men, not just for their position, but that a lot of men don't let it be known that a woman is as good as them, let alone better. I think we're very threatening to society and to the male in

general . . . the fact that he feels that he's got to be dominant, got to be
aggressive, that the little woman has to be protected and cared for and
taken care of . . .

This notion of male dominance and female helplessness is compounded by
few examples of strong women, and real fear of repercussions. As one
respondent explains:

I think every business I've been in has a paternalistic attitude. "We'll
take care of you." Bosses have even told me that. "Don't worry about it.
We'll take care of you." Of course they all lie. I don't know. Maybe it's
that I don't see that you have any real female heroes to look up to either.
I mean, you could look up to Rockefeller, and you wouldn't find the answer . . . There aren't that many women that are in the limelight and
the ones that are, are like the National Organization of Women, Equal
Rights Amendment, abortion rights, and that much publicity for a con-
troversial subject frightens a lot of people. I feel frightened at times
myself. If we have a press campaign and I know I'm going to be there,
and I know press people are going to be there, and there's going to be TV
probably, I wonder what my family and friends are going to think of
this. What's going to happen to me the next day at work?

Women's traditional family role was also seen as helping to perpetuate
sexism. Several women describe how these role expectations guide decisions women make. One realized the limitations of her career choice:

We've been geared by society, by the male population especially, that
we're suited for clerical work. We're suited for teaching and keeping
house. And the worst thing in the world would be for us to be piloting a
plane, or be on the board of directors for some corporation . . . My first
thought out of high school was, "I got to make some money and the best
way to do that is get some clerical skills and get a job as a secretary." I
didn't think about getting technical training in plumbing.

Another expressed frustration at society's expectation that women must
put their family roles first:

I think women are taught not to expect much still. You know, we're in
this great, wonderful, advanced age. Even now, you know, I see my
sisters coming out of high school, even the one that went to college, I just
see this attitude like you're going to come out of high school and you're
going to work a while and you're going to get married and have babies
and you'll do this your whole life and it's no use getting one of these high
level jobs because you're not going to do it. That's the thing that makes
me mad, but I don't know how to change it.

But that frustration is carried further when women become aware that despite their efforts to get good training for jobs, the power men have at the workplace still prevails. A woman with an Associate of Arts degree finds her job boring:

> I've got a degree and all . . . but I'm given the most mindless jobs to do. I'm totally bored. Yet, they tell me that without a degree, you know, I can't get any better. I know it's not true 'cause I go to school with a lot of men who have very good jobs who are just now getting their degree after years and years of work.

In fact, statistically speaking, she is correct. Women with college degrees earn essentially the same salaries as men with eighth grade educations.[17]

Another aspect of this frustration is expressed by one woman who throughout her interview expressed contradictory feelings about the roles of women and the necessity of activism, both her own and that of other women.

> There's always going to be differences between the sexes, but I don't want to feel that I don't have a chance because I'm a woman. Or that I wouldn't be as good as a man. I want to be looked at and base myself on being a person, and then, judging my capabilities and so forth from there. I don't want to be looked at as a woman — and she's got some capabilities. I want to be a person who's got a lot of things to give the world. I don't want to be judged by my sex alone. And I'd like to see women developed to the place where they are people . . . I'm not real aggressive. I'm not real militant. But I'd like to know that there's a position that was always looked at as a man's position, but I could walk into it without him having to think, well, what would it be like to hire a woman for this position. I'd like to be judged on my qualifications and my abilities, not my gender at all.

We can conclude that most respondents agree that male dominance and the ideology of sexism are significant factors that contribute to the devalued social position in which women find themselves. While most see this as perpetrated by men, others blame women for allowing it to carry on so successfully, and speak of the potential for women to unite to do away with this sort of self-denigration. This analysis applies both to job situations as well as to more general relationships between women and men, as the two following examples show us:

> . . . we haven't been willing to stand up for our rights . . . it's only been in the last twenty or thirty years that people are really taking a long, hard look at women and their role in society. And I'm not trying to

blame it all on the male society. I think women are just as much to blame as men if a woman sits back and takes abuse or puts up with not being promoted, or isn't willing to take on more responsibility just as the man who keeps her in that position. I think we need to be more aggressive through time and I don't think enough of us have stood together jointly to do that.

and:

I think it's our own fault. I think we've been only too happy to be patted on the head and told we're good girls. And we compete with each other for the attention of men. We cheapened ourselves, I think. I think we must have more sisterhood. I hate to be talking with a woman and she'll be paying full attention to you and suddenly a man appears . . . and suddenly this empty-headed little someone will immediately be coy, flirtatious, and leave you dangling. I think we've got to recognize each other some more.

When asked why women do this, the same respondent replied: ". . . When you know there's someone that's going to pick up the pieces, pay the rent . . . a girl doesn't have to think too much. I think so many of us are willing to spend our whole lives that way." Not surprisingly, we find both a consciousness of sexism and a willingness to admit that women buy into it, hoping for rewards in the form of security. For these respondents that situation necessitates an increase in solidarity with other women.

While consciousness of sexist ideology is high, there is little evidence that sexism is seen in structural terms, except for the experience of the immediate workplace. One respondent linked relationships between men and women to workplace structure:

I think men today don't want commitments, and I think women are beginning to realize this. More and more women are being left in the lurch. And we suddenly realize we don't have the skills to really help ourselves. I think our contribution is great. It's just never been recognized. I think . . . most employers pay us with the idea that, "Oh, their husband's paying the mortgage, they don't need much," and quite frankly, I always had that feeling that I didn't need very much. It was pin money.

Attitudes such as those expressed above led to another line of questions concerning the respondents' opinions of the women's movement. In addition, all were asked whether they thought Baltimore Working Women was part of the women's movement, to which there were mixed replies. In fact, some of the most contradictory statements were given in this section owing to different amounts of knowledge about the movement, different perceptions of it, and different levels of participation in it. We will see by their responses that consciousness pertaining to the women's movement is an aspect of feminist consciousness that may be contradictory.

Overall, the vast majority of respondents approved of the women's movement, though few ever participated in it in an active way. They often saw it as liberating women from restrictive sex roles and helping to change the public's attitudes toward women. In relating to men, one respondent suggested that the women's movement provided ". . . a more relaxed atmosphere. You can be normal. You can be human. You don't have to be the beauty queen." Several women expressed qualified approval based on their awareness that in its early stages the women's movement addressed problems primarily for young upper-middle-class women, leaving out women like themselves from the working class. Thus we see a consciousness about class permeating the attitudes of some respondents. They also saw the direction of the movement changing: "I'm in favor of it. Especially now that it's filtering down. You know, before I think mainly it was a middle and upper class thing. You know, not too many office workers would get into it. But now it's getting down to grass roots." An older woman expressed her approval of the movement, acknowledging the difficulty of adjusting to new ways of thinking and doing things at a later age: "I'm all for the women's movement. I think it's great, but sometimes I wish it hadn't happened in my lifetime, or so late in my lifetime, because if it had happened a generation ago, we'd all be so used to it." Consciousness about race also played a role for black women who, while approving of the movement for the most part, indicated that special issues concerning blacks rarely get addressed:

> . . . because the whites are in the majority, [our problems] are going to be second, or it's like ours is of little importance because there aren't enough of us to say, "Well, this is a problem." And then sometimes the problems are so subtle, it's like, even though we're in the same organization, they don't see it — other white women don't see it.

Some women explained that they didn't know much about the women's movement but felt that it was probably necessary. Others expressed disapproval of some aspects of the movement, a seemingly contradictory position on the surface, given their activism in a group fighting for the rights of working women. The following remarks exemplify this position. The first is from one of the most active members and an elected officer:

> I still like to be considered soft, and I like for my man to treat me like a lady, but I don't want to be treated as his equal in the sense that when

we go out on a date, or something like that, then it doesn't matter if he opens the door. To me, it matters . . . He's supposed to be the stronger one, so why not? But with the women's movement, it's getting men to like—"Well, I don't have to be bothered with any of those things anymore because they want to be treated equal." We want to be treated equal as far as our minds are concerned and not as far as man/woman. So for that, I don't like the women's movement totally.

Thus we find someone who can desire equality in one part of her life but not others, and has not embodied the essence of feminist consciousness. Yet she is a hard-working member of the organization, whose stated purpose for belonging is to help other women who work in offices.

A similar response was found in another active member, who earlier in the interview described an incident in her workplace in which she took a stand on the issue of sexual harassment against her boss, for which she was temporarily fired. Despite the risks she took and the militance of her behavior, she finds the women's movement as represented by NOW, too extreme:

A lot of NOW is hard-line, strict lines I couldn't warm up to. They were just so gung-ho, like *Ms.* magazine. I couldn't really enjoy it in and of itself because it was so hard-line. It's like having the extreme male chauvinist pig and the extreme liberated female. I'm not the extreme liberated female. I don't feel that I have to go burn my bra and call all men a pig . . . I think what they're doing is good and right but I don't think that NOW on the whole has to come across as heavy handed as they do sometimes . . . I'm not saying we should use the feminine wiles and ways to succumb people to us, but there's better ways of doing things than be known as the libbers who go out and burn bras and [I] think that a lot of the publicity that we get ends up turning back on us as negative publicity.

An officer of the organization was adamant in her separation of the group from her conception of the women's movement:

. . . I just think that the women's movement is just pitting man against woman and woman against man, whereas our organization is not like that. It's just work. We're just concerned about winning rights and respect and improving policies and to change policies and also to enforce the laws that are already existing. That's all we want to do. So the women's movement, I would say is a separate identity than Baltimore Working Women.

It is difficult to know how many of these statements are based on real knowledge of the movement and how many are speculation. Nevertheless, it is clear that it cannot be assumed that active involvement in a working women's organization is automatically an indicator of approval of the women's movement. This raises questions about our understanding of what constitutes feminist consciousness. Does disapproval of the women's movement represent a stand on women's equality, or is there a distortion in the respondents' understanding of feminism? Given the bad press the movement has gotten over the years, it is not surprising to find disapproval of it. Regardless, we must take these subjective views as seriously as those that approve of the movement, and try to understand the factors that lead to disapproval.

The apparent contradictions in attitude expressed here are not isolated cases. In her study of working class family life, Lillian Rubin examines the confusion faced by women who are both frustrated in their traditional roles and threatened by the possibilities of change represented by the women's movement.[18] She found no sense of solidarity among these women:

> Despite all the publicity generated by the women's movement about the dissatisfactions women experience in marriage, most workingclass women continue to believe that their feelings are uniquely theirs. Few have any contact with the movement or the people in it; few feel any support for their struggle from that quarter . . .[19]

Rubin reports mixed feelings about women's social position. Her respondents indicated support for equal pay for women for the most part, but they did not think women and men should compete equally for jobs. Throughout her study, Rubin found a conservatism and clinging to traditional family values that she explains as inherent in the overall insecure position in which the working class is found.[20]

Rubin also found that her respondents generally were ideologically opposed to women working outside the home for wages, yet, most of the women she met did so out of economic necessity. Once they were in the workforce, they often continued to work, finding it a relief from household drudgery.[21] They also liked the personal qualities of competence, importance, and independence gained through their jobs.[22] Most of these women had to juggle these positive aspects with traditional roles and expectations in the family, causing conflicts both within themselves and with other family members.[23]

Rubin's study involved women from similar class backgrounds as those found in this study. One major difference in the two populations is that all the respondents in my study work and, more importantly, participate collectively in a workers' organization. The difference in consciousness is, thus, not surprising. The similarities reveal conflicts women feel in the need to work and the traditional sex-role expectations.

It is important to note that opposition to the women's movement does not represent the majority opinion in this study. In fact, most respondents assumed that their organization was part of the women's movement, and were quite pleased about that affiliation. One woman discussed her somewhat contradictory feelings about being identified by co-workers as a "women's libber," for belonging to this organization:

> It's hard to live with the fact of a label like that, and on the other hand, it's very enjoyable to be labeled something because I wasn't in NOW before, and I wasn't very active before in women's groups and to be called that is sort of an honor. I feel — here I am, coming up from an office worker to a women's libber. I like the title. It's better than my actual title . . . Data Engineer. Women's libber I think is much more appealing to myself.

Several of those who saw the organization as part of the women's movement, also felt the group was too restrictive in its appeal to broader issues. One respondent suggested that the organization should include women in occupations other than office work, especially waitresses, believing that "equal rights encompasses all women." Yet she also thought that focusing on specific issues concerning office workers was a good strategy, given the size of the group and the magnitude of the problems women workers face. Others felt that the organization should actively work towards ratification of the Equal Rights Amendment, precisely because they see it as a women's organization. While the group supports the ERA, the activities of the organization have yet to focus on any issue broader than the workplace.

Many respondents expressed the belief that BWW was significant in terms of building solidarity among women, much as they had expressed that solidarity in terms of job consciousness. This solidarity was expressed in terms of new confidence and raised consciousness about women in general:

> I think it's made me more interested in the wider picture of what's happening to women, and makes me very, very sorry that I didn't jump into this when my husband died . . . And I had too many friends who made remarks about women and many thought that I had. I wasn't brave enough to just ignore what they would say. Y'know, about burning bras, or whatever.

Solidarity with other women is also seen as increasing women's creativity and ultimately their power. This is expressed as a confrontation with the oppressive conditions of sexism and the assumption that women cannot work together or wield power.

> I think it's important to establish a comradship between women who
> have been apart, that we can work together. And we are taught that we
> don't work together very well. And I think that when you get a group of
> women together you have a much more innovative, creative situation
> because we all, not only do we work full-time, we work full-time at
> home . . . we're very efficient.

Not only is this solidarity helpful to the women involved, it has an important effect in the public arena:

> It's a woman's organization, and I love to see women doing things.
> Women have sat back for so long and have been quiet and sedate and all
> of that . . . but to see women really wielding some power, that's excit-
> ing. And to see that these people are taking us seriously and they're
> afraid of us. You know, at the banks, all you do is mention [BWW] and
> they say, "Oh, my God. Get her out of here." You know, the govern-
> ment is calling us up for information.

This solidarity spans not only many workplaces in the city, but since the
organization is affiliated with a national movement, the membership can
then become aware of sharing problems and power with other women all
over the country. One staff person explained that she especially likes

> . . . the feeling of being part of a national movement . . . a lot of what
> happens to individuals when they get involved is they realize they
> weren't the only ones with the problem, which is a real powerful sort of
> realization. And then they realize that they could do something about
> some of those problems if they join together. And then there's the wider
> sense across the nation that women are doing the same kinds of things.

That BWW is a women's organization is very much in the consciousness of
the members, even for those who do not see it as part of the women's
movement. It represents a way to align themselves with other women to
take positive steps in building their knowledge, self-confidence and power
both as individuals and as a group. These notions are in the forefront of
their consciousness.

Objectively BWW is, in fact, a feminist organization, approaching
the problems of a specific area of sexism, the office. Yet, in confronting
such problems it must of necessity touch on a broader range of issues, particularly that of simply getting women to increase their confidence in the
context of a sisterly collective. The point here is, were it not a women's
organization, with special attention given to specific women's problems,
it simply would not have accomplished many of its goals. In fact, the
goals would more than likely have been quite different were men active in
the group.

THE RELATIONSHIP BETWEEN JOB
CONSCIOUSNESS AND FEMINIST CONSCIOUSNESS

The uniqueness of the special connection of woman-as-worker-as-woman gives rise to a broader form of consciousness encompassing more than the workplace and more than gender. In effect, because of the particular position these women hold, it can be argued that a consciousness anchored in their experiences both as women and as office workers prevails. Theoretically, capitalism and patriarchy, the structural conditions leading to this consciousness, affect women in a unique way so that

> *their special position as household workers outside of the wage-labor*
> *system, and their special position in the labor force—indicate the direc-*
> *tion necessary in a study of women's potential for class consciousness.*
> For if women's class position, like that of men, can be determined from
> their unique relationship to the production process, then their conscious-
> ness must also develop in relation to their experiences in the process.[24]

This relationship women have to capitalism and patriarchy contains within it a special set of contradictions inherent in the effects these two systems have on one another. This then leads to a special consciousness of women who experience both. At the most fundamental level, capitalism historically brought with it "bourgeois democracy," freeing women from slave status in the family to become free wage labor. Yet, this freedom cuts into the patriarchal structure of society, and affects women's influence in the family.[25]

> Capital's need for rationalization threatens patriarchal traditionalism.
> The most efficient use of women's labor power may demand that tradi-
> tions be changed. A wife's duties to her job may conflict with her duties
> to her work at home. As capitalism continues its struggle against a con-
> tinuously falling rate of profit, it must attempt to de-value labor power
> partly through the super-exploitation of women's labor power. Women
> are doubly exploited, first for their unpaid labor invested in the
> reproduction of labor power through their work at home, and second
> through their restricted position and lower salaries in the work force.
> But to maintain its income, the family is increasingly forced to send
> women into the labor force . . . This weakens the material basis of
> patriarchal power within the family by decreasing the economic depen-
> dence of women on men.[26]

Yet, capitalism also takes advantage of patriarchal traditions by employing women in the most devalued sectors of the workplace, considered to be "women's work" and even goes so far as to attempt to maintain patriarchal relationships between male bosses and female workers by imitating domestic relationships in the office, often at the expense of increased production and a more modernized bureaucratic system of control over the workplace.[27] Apparently the rewards of patriarchal control in the form of personal power over women office workers are still great enough for individual supervisors and bosses that they are reluctant to structure the office completely on the basis of bureaucratic control, which so pervades large companies.

Perhaps the most significant expression of the relationship of job consciousness and feminist consciousness is represented in the consistency with which respondents discussed the connections between their work lives and family lives. The decision to work, the type of work available or selected, the workplace issues these women were most concerned about, in one way or another were almost always tied to family experiences. Marital status, children, and husbands' concerns were all considerations in the work roles of these women. The consistency with which this was reported, unsolicited in any direct way, is an indication of how closely tied these are to life experiences and the consciousness of the respondents.

Almost all of the women, regardless of their marital status, age, or presence of children, indicated that their decisions about working were in one way or another tied to their present family conditions or future expectations. Whether single and independent, married with a working husband, divorced, separated, or widowed, most felt the necessity to earn money precisely because they could not rely on a man to provide an adequate income, or in many cases, any income at all. The problems become compounded for those women with dependent children, a large proportion of the membership:

> . . . [Now] they are running homes themselves, they have children . . . they're not just married, being taken care of. I don't think there's hardly any family where the woman can stay home anymore. Not that you wouldn't like to and that isn't a job in itself, but you have rent, you have cars, you have children and food.

Women without children understand this pressure:

> I'm a single woman with no children to raise, and if I lost my job, I'd find a way to get by . . . I'll do all kinds of wee little jobs to get by because I don't have a child to support — I've only got myself to think of, but I understand how some of these women feel. They've got kids to support . . . They don't have that man at home to bring home the paycheck.

Even women with good jobs express concern about the general condition of women's work and how it influences their options in relation to their family status: "I was lucky I had that job 'cause I had tried a couple of other places. I don't know how anybody can live on some of the salaries I was offered. With my kids, I probably would have had to stay married forever." From this testimony it is evident that it is not only by choice that women must consider their family status when coping with their worklife. An older women felt tremendous pressure to pursue a traditional relationship with a man: "I'm so frightened about this job. I've been here eight years, and in another two years I'll be vested in my pension. Big deal! Maybe when I'm 65 I can collect maybe $65 to $70 a month. So one part of me says I've got to find this man." Thus, we can see that many of the respondents perceive their job options and family conditions as mutually reinforcing, interdependent traps. This consciousness is further reinforced by a sexist ideology and the real power on the part of husbands and male employers to maintain traditional female roles at home and at work. Regardless of women's need or desire to work, the practice of sexism at home and at work limits women's opportunities. For example, several single respondents reported being asked about their dating habits, including one who was fired when her relationship with a man became entangled with her work life. It was also reported that fraternizing among employees is not allowed in many companies, and when it does occur, between male professionals and female clerical workers, the woman is more likely to get punished. There are other examples of this attempt to define women in terms of their family roles and punish them for it at the same time. One married, childless woman reports:

> I've run against the problem of people being nervous about my having a kid. My last boss was notorious for this. Every time I wasn't feeling well, he'd insist I was pregnant. He'd get upset because that meant that I was going to leave him. And I consider that an infringement on my privacy . . . and the other part of it was that he would assume that once I had a kid that was it, that I was only biding my time here. I wasn't really working because either I needed the money or for my own needs.

This relationship between male boss and female worker stands out because, even in their working relationship, male/female sex roles prevail. The role played by many women clericals is that of "office wife," or in some cases, a more overtly sexual role, but in either case it restricts the options for women. One office worker describes a co-worker, well liked by the male staff:

> She's just sweetness and light and it's part of her job, and I'm sure that's the reason why she got her job, because they thought this is the perfect woman, our little southern belle. The men are going to love her. She's

got a nice figure, she's very pretty, she's got this southern accent. The men will just eat her up.

But carrying out the traditional female role is not necessarily rewarded well:

I'm a legal secretary. I'm not supposed to think. The attorneys are the thinkers, which is most annoying, especially when—like the paralegals—I type something for them and I realize their grammar is so bad. I really do know a little bit more than they give me credit for and I used to sit on that job and feel, what can I do? It was the only thing I was trained to do many years ago. I married at 18.

In fact, female status is often used against her. One woman relates an altercation with her boss, cited in the preceding chapter, but worth repeating here:

. . . he started yelling at me because I couldn't understand it. "Could you explain it to me?" And then he started yelling. I said, "Well, I'm not hard of hearing. I just don't understand what you're saying." He said, "No, you're just dumb like all women. You need to be home washing dishes."

There was no consistency of opinion on whether women should stay home to raise children other than explaining that it depended on the individual woman's needs and interests. Most respondents believed that childrearing was an important job requiring skills, but poorly respected in the outside world. Employers rarely give women credit for experiences in childrearing and family maintenance. Respondents were also aware that that very lack of respect for women's traditional roles was a prime reason for their lack of power in the workplace:

Well, as you usually have, college degree vs. years of experience. I have thirty years' working experience. I have raised an entire family. That should tell you I'm quite competent to do something. But if you come in with a Master's Degree, and I've been holding the job three years, you will get the job. I will not get the job.

Several women felt strongly that marriage and children should interfere as little as possible in their work lives despite outside conditions that lend themselves to that interference. Some respondents discussed combining work and family life through part-time or temporary work. Most expressed interest in maintaining at least some financial independence as well as keeping outside interests while tending to family needs. Choice of careers throughout life are tied to the eventuality of family responsibilities. An editor explains:

> . . . one of the reasons I took the job was so that I could freelance when I raise a family . . . That was frankly the main consideration, that I did want a family at some point along the way, and I knew that I would go crazy if I didn't have something to do while . . .

Throughout the interviews, respondents expressed disappointment, if acceptance, at having their family roles define their work lives. But, there was no question that they saw the two very much interconnected. Many also used this understanding as their motivation for joining a working women's organization. Some faced specific job problems as a result of family situations. In one case, a problem arose concerning maternity leave and loss of position. Another woman felt troubled when her daughter lost her job, still another felt it difficult to discuss problems of sexual harassment with her boyfriend:

> You can't sit down with your boyfriend and explain your problems with sexual harassment, whereas another woman can deal with it, and can understand it. And the fact that it's a means to express and accomplish your inner thoughts regarding your problems in your situation, the lack of respect or the lack of rights that you think you have. It's a way of knowing you have feelings. It's an outlet for the emotions. For me it was a need to do something regarding it, and I had the feeling that I was being discriminated against in minor ways. They'd be minor to the individual, but when you're a woman and you deal with it throughout your life, it becomes very important . . . I've handled things better in my life since joining . . . because I'm working in positive steps to make things better. It might not be helping me directly, but it will help other women and eventually it will come back to me too.

In each case, these women sought support and concrete help in this organization. That other members had experienced this unique combination of family and work experiences couched in sexist practice and ideology enabled them to confront the problems in the context of the group. Again, we see that solidarity with others in the same situation is an important factor in choosing to join the organization. A newcomer explains:

> I came to more or less observe and to see if the organization was really sincere in its efforts for the common woman, so to speak, who has been out there trying to change the working conditions, or whether it was just another bureaucracy that was slowly being created to gobble up what its initial purpose was. And I think it's sincere.

Another woman had more specific reasons:

> I've always been interested in what was called the women's movement, because I always planned on making work a career, and it all came to a head in the winter when I was thinking about leaving my husband. I realized that I wouldn't be able to survive with a fulltime paycheck. I wanted to get together with other ladies and do something about that.

This solidarity also took the form of outreach to other women not already involved in the organization:

> A lot of opportunities are passed over to men because they assume that a woman is going to go home and stay with the babies. And we want to change that. We want them to realize that a large majority of us are self-supporting. We don't have anybody else doing it. We want to make a career in our lives. We basically want to inform people about the problems. We want them to know about the steps they can take. We want to draw attention to ourselves and get people involved in it and realize there's ways to fight the discrimination that goes on.

There was also expressed the hope that efforts taken by the organization would make it easier for the next generation to cope with working life, if not this generation:

> . . . not everyone knows that banding together means that it's going to help them in the long run. You may not see the effects of it right now, but who knows? Your children or your grandchildren may see this, and so that's [how I see] my purpose up here, in Baltimore Working Women. I may not see the effects, but hopefully, when I'm dead, my children or your children may see them.

The concepts of job consciousness and feminist consciousness have been developed here to show the uniqueness of the combination of circumstances in which women office workers live and work. It is not enough to look only at job-related experiences and attitudes when examining the consciousness of any worker. Nor is it sufficient to analyze women's experiences only in terms of their sex roles, if that were even possible. We must look at specific job structures and what kind of worker fills those positions if we want a good understanding of their consciousness. Neither the designation of class by traditional Marxist theory nor a feminist theory of patriarchy fully explain any given set of workers' experiences and beliefs. We must combine these theoretical orientations, seeing both job and gender as critical factors in the development of consciousness. The overlapping of these two areas is apparent to the respondents in this study, who consistently draw relationships between their experiences as women at work and in their personal lives, particularly their families. I do not think these women are unique in doing this, nor are such observations limited to women or to office workers only. Rather, it is the social scientist who has been remiss by ignoring these factors that so consistently combine with one another, thus missing the whole point of what it means to be a woman office worker.

Only if we see these factors in combination can we understand the development of the working women's movement, its particular direction, and the unique forms consciousness and solidarity take. A strong case has been made here for establishing the base of consciousness in the workplace and the gender of the worker. In considering the next stage, class consciousness, these factors will continue to be vital to this analysis.

CLASS CONSCIOUSNESS

The third type of consciousness, class consciousness, addresses the respondents' perceptions of their particular conditions as women office workers in the context of the working class as a whole. Class consciousness is a vital element in understanding historical change. It is also a difficult concept to grasp as it relies on the subjective understanding of the conditions in which workers find themselves, as do the other types of consciousness discussed in this study. Marxists and non-Marxists alike agree that the force and direction of workers' movements of all kinds, from conservative unions to militant revolutions, depend upon the subjective interpretation of the objective working conditions.[28] While scholars have spent much energy defining class consciousness and placing it into general theory about social change, little attempt has been made to apply the concept to the actual (as opposed to assumed) ideas and behavior of workers themselves. Except for some quantitative surveys of work dissatisfaction, workers themselves have had little opportunity to formally express their ideas about their place in society. These surveys are primarily in the form of short-answer questionnaires that do not give respondents much leeway in self-expression, thus limiting the potential for them to express or explain various and possible contradictory thoughts. There have been some good journalistic studies done[29] that, in fact, bring out a broader range of subjective experiences due to the open-ended nature of the interviews, but the analysis of the information provided is primarily left up to the reader. The absence of a methodical, scientific study of class consciousness has made it even more difficult to apply theory to reality. Theoretically, there is general agreement that class consciousness progresses from identification with smaller units to larger ones, until it encompasses the entire working class. It is also assumed that as one becomes more class conscious, the potential for militant action against the capitalist class increases, although this action may take a variety of forms.

An additional problem that results in part from the lack of thorough investigations into workers' consciousness results from the difficulty of applying theoretically consistent ideas to the complexities of social reality. While class consciousness progresses logically in theory from one stage to the next, in fact it is full of contradictions both in the attitudes of the workers as well as their behavior. One must apply an understanding of dialectical process here in the subjective arena as well as in our understanding of the objective historical progress of modern capitalism. Since we have had little access to the opinions of workers, it is no wonder that we have difficulty understanding their actions on the job, their awareness of working-class interests and their level of interest in labor organizing. While there has been some interest in this in the industrial sector, even less attention has been given to white-collar workers and to the special experiences of women in the workplace. Thus, the unique experiences of women office workers may contribute to a mixed consciousness that does not run smoothly from one stage to the next, but offers its own dialectical combination whose progress is unique to that group of workers.

Michael Mann, in his book, *Consciousness and Action Among the Western Working Class*, has defined four elements of class consciousness that are especially useful and lend themselves to operationalization for the purposes of this study. Mann summarizes:

> Firstly, we can separate class *identity* — the definition of oneself as working-class, as playing a distinctive role in common with other workers in the production process. Secondly comes class *opposition* — the perception that the capitalist and his agents constitute an enduring opponent to oneself. These two elements interact dialectically; that is to say opposition itself serves to reinforce identity, and vice-versa. Thirdly is class *totality* — the acceptance of the two previous elements as the defining characteristics of (a) one's total social situation and (b) the whole society in which one lives. Finally comes the conception of an *alternative* society, a goal toward which one moves through struggle with the opponent.[30]

Each element described above will be discussed in the context of the findings of this study. The development of class consciousness is part of a continuum whose foundation is job consciousness and feminist consciousness that have been found to be intricately connected. The interplay between these types of consciousness and the development of activism and solidarity contribute to an even greater consciousness. To understand to what

degree members of Baltimore Working Women experience class consciousness is the ultimate purpose of this chapter.

Class Identity

The research thus far has shown that the participants in this organization categorically have a strong identity with other women office
workers. In some cases, the identity with female status is the most strong.
In other cases, it is the job with which they most closely identify. For
most, it is a relatively equal mixture. Both in terms of objective circumstances and subjective experience, the status of office work is equated
with that of the position of women. This well-documented consciousness
is crucial to the creation of organized efforts to improve the working conditions of this particular sector of the workforce. There is a theoretical
premise that is made in the classical literature that consciousness is limited
only to a small sector of the working class if the participants' identity goes
no further than identity with a particular job (and, in this case, gender).
It is thus important to investigate the degree to which those women identify with the working class as a whole, or again, in Mann's words, consider ". . . the definition of oneself as working class, as playing a distinc-
tive role in common with other workers in the productive process."[31]

There was not a single case of a respondent making an unqualified
identification with the working class. That is to say, identity was always
tied to gender and/or office work. An occasional remark indicated an
identification with workers in other areas of production, but this occurred
only if the respondent was pressed to make that identification. Nevertheless, the association with working-class women overall was fairly strong,
as the following comments indicate. One respondent was asked to
describe the membership of the organization, and saw it as representing
women of the working class:

> It's working women. It's people, they are working and they're just every-
> day people. In normal menial, low-paying jobs, and they're devoting
> part of their free time to this organization which has not had much fund-
> ing and it's not a whole lot of professional people. There's no spokes-
> person saying this is the way it ought to work who has no personal ex-
> perience. People who are running the campaigns know what they're
> talking about because they're working in the jobs every day or they had
> working jobs before or their sister or mother or their kids are working
> the jobs.

The above comment was representative of the appreciation many
members had that the organization was run by people who were office
workers, and knew firsthand what that work was like. The importance of

being in an organization whose leadership has the same class background, who can genuinely identify with the rank and file, is significant. It represents an awareness that shared consciousness derived from class-based experience is important to participants. Such comments are similar to those made earlier in this chapter concerning recent changes in the women's movement towards a closer identification with working class women. Membership in the organization has clearly affected the consciousness of the women involved who recognize at least in part the structural base of class differences, in that they realize that problems they face go beyond individual differences:

> . . . I work in a bank now, and I've sort of . . . hopped from division to division within the bank and I see sort of a difference between divisions, how women are treated . . . I don't know whether it's because I've been in the organization so long since my awareness has been increased and I can see the different forms of discrimination happen. I don't know exactly what the answer is to that. I see discrimination all around me. It's terrible. An example: . . . I have a boss who has difficulty, even though I've been in his employ almost a year, he has difficulty remembering my name. I'm serious. So I think all women in the division or the department, or whatever, are treated sort of the same way, one of the girls. They're called hon. They're called dear, sweetie pie.

Several respondents indicated an identity with women who, while formally affiliated with management, had questionable class identity because they were women. A description of a female manager:

> She's been there twenty-five years . . . I consider her more of a worker than a manager too, because she's been there twenty-five years and I think she's another token woman manager and I'd love to know what kind of money she makes, because I've got a feeling she's not making that much.

The awareness that there is a questionable gray area of class position for many workers because they are women is clearly present, and helps explain the apparent lack of class identity with men.

Race is also a consideration. One black office worker explains that black women face particular problems on the job, yet their gender is equally important in considering job discrimination: ". . . they aren't making the bucks that anybody else is. When you even talk about black men, black men down at Bethlehem Steel make more money than a white woman doing any clerical position."

The degree to which respondents limit their class identity to working-class women rather than the working class as a whole is significant. It is evident that this identification is not with women of all classes, as we have evidence that it has strong ties to the working class as represented by identity with clerical workers. But that identity is not brought into the realm of male-dominated production areas either. This finding is indicative of the impact of gender indentification, a result of sexist ideology and patriarchal practices in the consciousness of the respondents. We can assume that any form of class identity among these women will be heavily affected by the prevalence of patriarchy.

> . . . although capitalism has itself eroded patriarchy and has brought into being movements and ideas which are both anti-capitalist and anti-patriarchal, it still maintains the subordination of women as a group. Patriarchy has continued in capitalism as an ever present prop in time of need. Although women are not literally the property of men, the continuation of female production in the family means that women have not yet even won the right to be exploited equally. The wage system in capitalism has continued to be structured according to the assumption that women's labour is half that of men on the market. Behind this is the idea that women are somehow owned by men who should support them. Women are thus seen as economic attachments to men, not quite as free labourers. Their wage is still seen as supplementary . . . This very simple economic fact about the position of women in capitalism acts as a bribe to keep women with men.[32]

The question whether gender identity is seen as an interference with the working class or is rather a significant, but not detracting piece of that identity, based on objective experiences in the world of work is important. I would argue that as long as patriarchy prevails at work and in the family, the class identity of working-class women will be characterized by gender identity. This does not lessen their class identity but rather creates a gender-specific class identity that is the taking-off point for consciousness among this sector of workers. The same subjectivity that allows workers in general to identify with each other against capitalists operates to help women workers find their own place in the working class. This does not interfere with their class identity as a whole but puts it in a specific dimension based on the experiences of patriarchy and sexism.

In a discussion of fractions, or divisions in the working class, which may apply in this case to women workers, Edwards points out that while it may appear that different sectors of workers are acting solely in their own interest, we must be cognizant that self-interest is motivated on the foundation of class relations:

> The point here is not that these fractions have "betrayed" the class cause. Far from it; they have acted upon class-rooted oppression as that oppression has been specifically experienced by each fraction . . .

> . . . each working-class fraction presses upon the state its political priorities, and capitalists, from a more entrenched position, do likewise. But the underlying material (class) relations ensure that the interests of each working-class fraction come into conflict primarily with the interests of capitalists, and so the chief adversary of each class fraction is not another fraction within the working class but rather the business community.[33]

Theoreticians of class consciousness may see this as a division within the working class in conflict with a more total identification but this view only indicates their refusal to see gender as a significant subjective factor in the lives of workers.

> The Left continues to view women in general, and women workers even more, as adjuncts to the male proletariat. No autonomous revolutionary role has been envisioned for women workers within the Marxist tradition. Women workers have been seen as especially exploited, especially dominated, especially oppressed, but never in a situation with unique and sharp contradictions which would create the potential for a revolutionary outlook.[34]

This interpretation of women's position is unfortunate, as it must surely limit the development of a thorough understanding of working-class life for both women and men, particularly in terms of understanding their family experience. One wonders if men in the industrial workforce are expected to have a strong identity with women clerical workers or, in fact, housewives, before they are considered to have class consciousness. Further, it can be argued that traditional examinations of class consciousness ignore issues related to gender, so that the consciousness of male workers is seen as the basis of all class consciousness. In fact, we may find that working-class men have equally strong gender identification if we were to look for it.

Class Opposition

Mann describes class opposition as ". . . the perception that the capitalist and his agents constitute an enduring opponent to oneself."[35] In the case of this element of class consciousness, we again find some concentration of gender identification, though not as strong as in the case of class identity. Perhaps because it is assumed most employers are men, descriptions of their position vis à vis the capitalist class are less likely to contain specific elements pertaining to patriarchy. A moderate proportion of respondents showed direct awareness of class opposition. For instance, several respondents indicated that the power of large corporations, particularly banks, limited their own control over their lives. Some of this knowledge was gained through participation in the organization: "I've learned that the banks are the key decision-makers of our economic society, which I didn't have any idea of before. I also learned the idea that once your money is deposited, then the banks can do anything they want with the money." A staff-member clarifies this awareness among members:

> It seems to me in talking with people that the little control that most of us have over our work lives is a real problem in the long run because what I was saying about profits, that companies want to make demands, that people have very little control. I would like to see that changed.

Some respondents disliked the maldistribution of wealth, yet they did not see themselves in opposition to capitalists since, for them, that opposition meant approval of communism: "I don't believe in, like, people being rich at the expense of other people, but there's nothing wrong with capitalism. Communism promised to bring them [the rich] down, but, you know, people in communist countries are poor there, and no better off than our poor." Perhaps the most consistent indication of class opposition came from those who believed the reason they, as women office workers, got paid low wages was the profit system under which capitalists benefit. In these cases, we find strong ties, once again to gender, as a significant factor: ". . . they have women in those low paying jobs. And it's like a hidden asset, actually. That's part of their profits, by keeping them low paid . . . but tough . . . they will have to cut down on their profit. They'll have to find another way because it's tough for women too." Another respondent discussed this problem in relation to the difficulty of passing the Equal Rights Amendment. She believes that the passage of this amendment would "be more effective" than present laws: "Maybe that's why there's so much resistance to it. It's going to have more clout. And it's going to cost business money."

Several women pointed out that men tend to fare better than women in terms of pay because they are often organized in unions, or simply because they are men. Talking about the issue of the relation between low pay for women and the profits of large companies, one respondent explains:

> Businesses want to save money. That's where they think they can save money . . . I don't think it's particularly directed at women. It's just the way it worked out. But that's why I'm very happy in trying to push . . . male secretaries, male bank clerks . . . because if you get them in on the right level . . . then we can maybe see something.

A few respondents described class opposition that included women as part of the capitalist class, an indication that gender was not always tied to class identity:

> I found that some women have gone ahead in the business world and have worked their way up to the top; sometimes they're our enemy too. Because they forget where they came from . . . and many times those women treat their clerical help and their secretaries worse than the men. And I think that that's something we're really going to have a hard time dealing with.

It was also understood that women in managerial positions are used to give the impression that women have promotional opportunities, as well as trying to ameliorate the divisions between women clerical workers and male bosses:

> They'll have a few token women . . . [who] make a good salary so that they can get the women working in lower paid jobs to say, "Well, look, I work there. It's not all that bad. I was a secretary once. I worked for your boss and he's really not that bad. Try to understand."

An additional source of information on class opposition is the way in which members of the organization perceive the responses of their families, friends, co-workers, and employers to their participation in the group, as well as their perception of the general public image the organization holds. This is helpful because in describing these perceptions, sources of conflict are often indicated.

There were mixed feelings on the part of respondents about the perceptions of family and friends concerning their participation in the organization. In some cases the response is considered positive, in others negative. Of those that are negative, some take the form of teasing the participant about feminism or militance. Several women have tried to bring friends or co-workers to meetings, most of whom refused because of family obligations or other activities. The respondents whose families or friends disapproved explained that this disapproval did not interfere with their participation. A young woman about to be married described her fiance's attitude toward her active participation in the organization in terms of opposition to her fiance's class position:

> Right now he has some negative feelings. He's very much a company man . . . whatever the company does is right. I just plain came out and said, "I'm out to destroy people like you. And if you're involved, you're going to get hurt. I'll picket your company. I feel that if a company is discriminating against half of its employees, it's not right, and I'm sure going to speak up about it. If you're in the middle, if you didn't speak up, that's tough."

When asked if her position created any conflict between them, she replied, "No, he'll drive me to the meetings and pick me up. He's never come to any. Of course, probably he'll feel lost . . . around a hundred women."

Most respondents believed their employers saw their membership in the organization as a threat. Some women respond to this perception by not letting their employers or co-workers know about their participation, and hope they do not find out through some other means, for fear of being fired.

One participant explained that the isolation most women feel in their offices increases their fears. Being the only member of the organization in her office forces her to examine the precarious position she is in: "Why don't they [co-workers] see this? Why am I the only one? That's the point I'm facing. I start to look at myself as the rabble rouser in the office." Another woman refused to let those fears intimidate her. She argued that she has a right to participate without fear of reprisal:

> A number of women worry about being seen on the corner by their boss while they're leafleting—but don't. You can't work from fear of repercussions on that. If he works for his country club to try to get the golf membership up, or try and do whatever he wants, that's his business the same as it's your business. I have, in leafleting, run across employers while I was standing there, and when I got back to the office I was asked what I was doing, and what it was for, and promptly handed them a leaflet, and they understood.

Those who have let it be known they belong to the organization have received mixed responses. For one woman, the knowledge of her membership by the staff had immediate effect on work roles: ". . . when I started working there I was telling the other woman in the office about Women Employed [former name], and they [male supervisors] all heard about that and they said, 'Oh well, we're not going to cross her.' So they asked her [the other woman] to make the coffee." Some respondents believe their bosses were intimidated by their participation in the group, fearing that the group might use office space and work time to hold meetings, or worse, that the group might direct activities against their place of employment. One common response of male employers was amusement, a response the participants hope to eliminate by increasing their effectiveness:

> I'd like the day to come when we have enough clout that when my boss sees one of our leaflets, he won't laugh, because the first leaflet which I saw which made me join Baltimore Working Women, I brought it right in the office . . . I looked at it and said, hey, wow, we need something

like this. And I was very impressed by the banking results, and I said, this group must have something together — I want to get in on this. And I immediately took it over to . . . my . . . boss . . . and I said, "Isn't this impressive? Maybe they should do this to insurance companies too." And he just gave me this coy smile and walked away. You know, like, "Oh, that's nothing." But I'd like to see his reaction if they did start investigating insurance companies . . .

Consciousness about their employers' reactions to the organization, whether it is perceived as amusement, fear, or attempts at intimidating the employee, clearly indicates that one's membership in the group stands in opposition to the interests of one's employer. Respondents also were aware that the organization had a significant impact on local companies, owing to their public activities and profuse favorable press coverage. The overall assumption is that these companies were surely more powerful than a working-women's organization, but while there is real inequality of power and fear of potential reprisals, the position of underdog could also be used in favor of working women. As one activist put it: ". . . it looks bad to have this small organization of lowly office worker women challenging the big male-dominated bank with *all* this money. It looks bad." Most agree that the large local companies see the organization as a threat. One woman expressed discomfort with this notion: "That's something I've found hard to deal with since I've joined the organization. People are actually afraid of you. I mean, not people in the street, but companies, like banks." Another thought this fear was useful: "The employers can see that women are banding together to try and change things. That may be intimidation on our part towards them, which doesn't hurt."

When asked why the organization is seen as a threat, most saw it in terms of the success of the campaigns, the favorable publicity it has received, and its overall uniqueness:

. . . it's new. Women organizing is new. And we're getting things accomplished and I think that's surprising. They don't know where we're going to strike next . . . I don't really think we're posing any threat to anybody. I just think that what people find threatening is that we're serious. And we're not going to go away. We're going to keep agitating until we get what we want.

The above comments are indicative of a mixed understanding of the way in which office workers and bosses stand in class opposition to one another. The respondent perceives some opposition, but also its resolvability within the context of class relations as they are, which is fairly representative of the opinions of most of the respondents. Analysis of their class position rarely goes further than working towards better working conditions, pay and promotion policies, and respect on the job. For this reason, their ability to reach the third stage, class totality, is limited.

Class Totality

There is no indication that their position on women's work roles as part of the working class permeates their lives in the way Mann has described: "the acceptance of the two previous elements as the defining characteristics of (a) one's total social situation and (b) the whole society in which one lives."[36]

The lack of this level of analysis is not surprising, as it is rarely exhibited in any American class or class fraction. Lack of access to critiques of class relations in the workplace or society as a whole is an important factor. Few people have access to class analysis, thus they frame their perceptions of their environment in available traditional analyses, which tend not to be critical of the existing order. Nevertheless, the potential for developing this is present, given the extent of class identity and class opposition already described. It would not be surprising that if this class totality were to develop it would carry the gender-specific themes described in the expression of class identity.

The degree to which members experience class identity and class opposition as class totality may in part be understood by their opinions of labor unions. The acceptability of unions to these women would indicate a certain degree of solidarity with an acceptable vehicle through which to gain power in the workplace, as a collective effort of workers against their employers. Thus, class identity and class opposition are combined. While this in and of itself does not represent class totality as defined by Mann, it does represent a move in that direction.

Overall, most respondents approved of labor unions, although there were several qualifiers that were significant. Generally speaking, they saw unions as potentially helpful, as they recognized that unions have helped workers oppose the power of their bosses in many respects: ". . . don't you think that if it wasn't for the unions we'd still be working fourteen hours a day, we'd still have child labor? I don't think the rich industrialists gave up all this of their own accord, out of the goodness of their hearts. I think they were forced to."

Recognition of class opposition is clearly of central importance in their approval of unionization. The staff is aware that there are many women clerical workers in the city, whose fathers and husbands are in unions and would probably favor them, who they hope to attract to the organization. In fact, several respondents acknowledged that men in their families were union members and this close association made them both more knowledgeable about unions and more favorably disposed toward going in the direction of unionization themselves. One woman whose brothers and father belong to unions, as well as many of her neighbors, had strong feelings about misinformation she has heard about them. She described a lecture she attended in which unions were accused of driving prices up and generally ruining the country:

> I just sat there and steamed . . . He made it like the unions are wrong. The people are getting rich off unions, and I thought, I know a lot of people in my old neighborhood . . . it's very heavy industry. A lot of people working are in unions and none of them are rich. None of them live half as nice as that lawyer does, you know . . . My father, he's got a house, but he don't got a fancy house. They make enough to get along . . . union workers do well, but I don't see too many of them walking around with a thousand dollars in their pockets.

Another activist with a union background had mixed feelings about unions:

> I think they're a necessary evil. I think they also have their politics and maybe parts of them are not all for the worker . . . But my father, I guess it stems back when he organized the furriers' union, and I learned quite later that he was even put in jail . . . there were a lot of abuses in industry and so it was needed to be done.

Some respondents are in unions at their workplace, and a few have taken an active role in their unions. They saw significant positive changes in their working conditions as a result of unionization. One union activist describes her workplace prior to unionization: "I was typing and there were so many terrible things there—like they wouldn't let you go to the bathroom. You couldn't comb your hair. And they would time you and things like that. So that is when I started getting active . . ." She described some of the advantages of her present union: "Definitely we don't have to go and make coffee and things like that. And we have a grievance procedure up there. We don't have to put up with sexual harassment. There are definite advantages of having a group to work for you." But most have had no direct experience with unions. Several respondents indicated that it is office workers who are presently in the most need of unions. One woman explained her support because she saw the lack of unionization as a set back in progress for office workers, while others have benefitted from unionization: "We are so behind in a lot of . . . areas. I think if we did unionize initially and did try and use the pull of the numbers that we could make the major changes that should have been made fifty, sixty years ago." Another, who joined Baltimore Working Women because she felt it particularly served the purpose of a union in part, described insecure working conditions as the major reason for unionizing the office: ". . . I always felt that office workers should be unionized 'cause I don't think they have too much security; that they can be fired on the spot . . . And I always felt, like, what have they got? Who do they go to for their problems?" Respondents are fully aware of the impact of unions on employers, even if unionization is only suggested: "Oh, union! That word scares them so much. They tried it at . . . and I heard management was having a fit." Several women experienced attempts at intimidation by employers where unions were actively starting an organizing effort. It is not unheard of to be threatened with firing. A conversation about union organizing exemplifies respondent's knowledge about the interplay between unions, workers, and employers:

> A. One of the supervisors was collecting all the [leaflets].
> B. [They] took it out of the employees' hand as they came in the door. Couldn't you put it in your bag so they didn't see it and run in the ladies room and . . . ?
> A. . . . don't you think the fact they do get scared, like, this is a good sign?
> B. . . . people used to come around and try to unionize us and hand out leaflets. Every time they tried to start a union we got a raise.
> A. Tell them to come in once a month!

Several women expressed an interest in strikes and mass demonstrations. One woman who works for a university where secretaries are beginning to unionize believed public action would be helpful: "I was there in the '70s when the students demonstrated out on Charles Street to stop Viet Nam and that's what I would like to see. I would like to see the secretaries get out there. Stop traffic. Put up big banners. And really get somebody's attention." One woman who believes that few people recognize the importance of office work expressed it this way: ". . . if, God forbid for this country, they did go on strike, I think we'd make the changes we need to a lot quicker than the means that we're using now." Yet she did not see this as an effort that would be identified with the working class as a whole, whom she thought were much better off than clerical workers:

> For most workers I don't think it's necessary because I don't think most workers are overlooked the way clerical positions are . . . I'm not trying to say that their unions are not worthwhile . . . I'm just saying that of all the organizations of all the groups of workers that I can look at today in society, I think the one that needs to be unionized is the secretary and clerical worker.

This argument is a good example of consciousness based once again on this particular sector of the working class, and not class consciousness as a whole. It also shows us that militance and activism are not confined to those who are class conscious in the classic meaning of the term, and can be exhibited as well by those whose consciousness is more specific to a particular group.

Not all respondents were so enthusiastic about unions. Many members expressed mixed feelings about their effectiveness, or at least some reservations. Seeing them as "a necessary evil" was one way of describing them. Fearing the power of unions was a common thought — that one should be skeptical that they will accomplish what they say they set out to do: "I think there are a lot of instances where they help, but a lot of them seem to get out of hand. It seems to be the union heads that are running things instead of the people that make up the union." This skepticism is often centered around the bad record male-dominated unions have in terms of women's issues and their reluctance to organize women or clericals. One union supporter explains:

> I just know that our unions are mostly men, too. A lot of times they are not sensitive to women's needs either, and we have to make them more aware. But it's better than nothing, I'll tell you that. At least I'm in a union . . . and I'm making equal pay on the job.

Skepticism about the advantages of unions for women was further expressed by the same respondent in terms of the expected roles of men and women:

> . . . Why are they all men in the unions as executive president or whatever? Why are they men? Because men don't go home after work . . . Their wife is there. She can take care of the house, kids, fix dinner and everything. They just go to the union meetings. They have the time to do it and everything. And they're insensitive because they're not helping their wife. Men just think still, in their minds, that they can do everything. That women can be working and going home and taking care of everything else, too . . . both people are working, right? And they should take care of everything. Union men are the same way. They just go out after work and have their union meeting and that's really good, but the same union woman here at work has to go home and take care of her family.

Several people brought up specific issues of concern to women that unions have historically ignored, centering around family needs, especially day care. For women with low pay and terrible working conditions that skepticism can only be alleviated with a proven good track record. One respondent explains:

> I'm all for unions but I don't know that they're good for all women
> workers. If you're only bringing home a hundred dollars a week you're
> going to have to pay something to a union each month. How much good
> is that going to do you? I think if you could belong to a powerful union,
> something like an AFL-CIO that had a branch for clerical and office
> staff, that would be beneficial. But like the one they tried to get at
> _____ Bank that no one heard of — I think that was the problem.
> Nobody heard of that union and the people that had, it had a reputation
> of being ineffective.

In her study of the telephone company, Elinor Langer describes responses
of women during a union drive which reiterate these points:

> . . . what about free dental care, medical check-ups, low cost car-
> purchasing programs: Some issues were raised that were more basic.
> They were women and they were being raided by men. They would be
> asked to walk out to support the men. Would the men walk out to sup-
> port them? Why were there no women in the top positions in the union
> when 45 percent of the members were women? Why did women's sal-
> aries in the company start at $79.50 when the lowest amount paid to a
> man was $95.00?[37]

The very structure of unions provides a form of control that often works to
the advantage of capitalism and patriarchy, leaving the needs of women
members unaddressed:

> Trade unions play a dual role within capitalism. The official structure of
> the union is partially integrated into the state and enables the employer
> to calculate and plan, reducing spontaneous local militancy. But the
> union organization at the shop floor contains an implicit attack on
> private profits and the control of capital over labour power. Centraliza-
> tion on a national level brings strength but it also means that the
> workers' creation, the union, can pass out of the control of the rank and
> file. This is particularly true of women because there are very few
> women represented at the top of unions and women are not often
> militantly organized at the base. Also the whole orientation of the trade
> unions is masculine. It is only by a special effort that men remember
> women. The only guarantee women have that their own interests will be
> considered is to organize as workers *and* as women.[38]

A few women believed that an organization like Working Women is
preferable to a union and could also be used to keep unions in check concerning issues specific to women:

> I think we should stay on the outside just so we can serve as a watchdog
> for the unions too. Because it seems to me that they could take us in and

do basically the same thing as big business has done . . . not do a whole
lot for the female worker.

At the time of this study, a number of active members were aware
that the national organization with which the group is affiliated was
negotiating affiliation with a union, but the details of that possibility
were not well known to the general membership.* The overall feeling was
that the rank-and-file members had to be gradually introduced to the idea
of unionization, as it was expected that they may leave the organization if
unionization is emphasized too much:

I know that the word "union" really scares a lot of young women . . .
Not all Baltimore Working Women feel that we should be unionized so
why should I go around starting that. But I do know that the national
organization is talking to unions, so maybe something will gradually
evolve.

Interestingly enough, the issue of unionization was never raised at
any meeting, event or informal discussion in which I participated, and it
was explained to me that this was purposeful, so as not to pose a threat to
participants. Nevertheless, when attending a national event, the summer
school of 1980, there was an unusually heavy emphasis on unions, with
the main thrust being the necessity for office workers to unionize. There
was also much attention given to the need to keep that unionization focused on the special needs of women office workers. The response to this
new emphasis on those who attended with whom I spoke was essentially
the same as the general view of unions as already discussed. The generally
favorable view of unions, with reservations directed toward gender issues,
is consistent with other class-related attitudes found in this study. The
degree to which we can speculate about class totality from these findings
is again tied to job- and gender-specific consciousness.

It is important to re-examine the concept of class totality in terms of
gender, as we have the two previous indicators of class consciousness,
identity and opposition. If one includes the concept of gender-specificity
as part of class totality, we find a much better case for arguing the potential for class totality among participants. In fact, the strong connection
these women make between family roles and job experiences indicates a
sophisticated conscious integration of their private and public worlds.
Marxists point out that with the development of modern industrial
capitalism, the worker finds himself (here I am deliberately specifying
male gender) living and working in two separate and often contradictory

---

*Working Women has since affiliated with The Service Employees International Union.

spheres; the private world of the family and the public world of the work-place. This very separation contributes to worker alienation and dissatis-faction, but in and of itself, not necessarily to consciousness and action. The awareness of the separation and resulting contradictions is crucial to the development of class consciousness, according to Marxists. If this is the case, women who work both in the home and outside it, and whose iden-tity as females is found there, are in a unique position to develop that con-sciousness. This experience of working inside and outside the home is de-scribed by some as a "dual shift":

> The dual-shift situation for women is a most important factor in ad-dressing her class consciousness, for it is part of the *uniqueness* of her position under capitalist patriarchy . . . Woman's position in two realms of work as opposed to one, and the differences between these realms (which both have "use-value" to capitalism and to patriarchy), provide even more potential for contradictions to arise.[39]

That more and more working class families are dependent upon the income of two adults to keep them out of poverty increases the pressure on women to work outside the home while maintaining traditional family roles, thus increasing the likelihood of consciousness. Male counterparts to this development have not for the most part altered their traditional par-ticipation in the family, and thus are in essentially the same position of alienation as they were before their wives worked for wages outside the home.

The ever-present identity with family roles has tremendous impact on life outside the home, both voluntarily (choices made about working) and involuntarily (low wages, sex-segregated jobs, lack of promotions, sexual harassment, for example). "Marxists are well aware that the seg-mentation of life in capitalist society constitutes an obstacle to the realiza-tion of class consciousness. For the latter to develop, the worker must make 'connections' between his work and his family life and between his industrial and his political activity."[40] The nature of women's participa-tion in these two worlds of work and family puts them in a position of greater receptivity to developing a sense of class totality.

Conception of an Alternative Society

Among the definitions of class consciousness examined in preparation for this research, several include a specific conception of an alternative society. Others limit their description of class consciousness to an aware-ness of shared experiences with people of the same class, as well as some form of opposition to other classes or the ruling class.[41] Most also indicate some sort of activism associated with class interests such as strikes or union participation as representative of class consciousness.[42] Mann describes the most progressive step in class consciousness as a "conception of an alternative society" as "a goal toward which one moves through struggle with an opponent."[43] As a Marxist, Mann describes the development of this level of class consciousness as a growth of awareness created dialectically, as contradictions in one's experience as a worker clash with ideas about the way society should operate:

> Consciousness grows (some Marxists say it "explodes") as the worker links his own concrete experience to an analysis of wider structures and then to alternative structures. It is in this sense that Marxism is a materialist theory: contradictions within the sphere of production and the growth of collective power are experienced by the worker before he generalizes a theory of socialism.[44]

Of course, this conception of an alternative society has its base in classical Marxist theory that sees class relations progressing in dialectical fashion in the context of class conflict toward a socialist society. Charles Anderson summarizes Marx's theory of class consciousness:

> Class consciousness is simultaneously revolutionary consciousness, for it understands the source of alienation and material bondage to be in the capitalist mode of production, and that capitalist relations must be replaced by socially organized, controlled and utilized production. Class consciousness of the bourgeoisie is an outmoded, false consciousness under developed capital. Class consciousness in the proletariat is a consciousness of material reality, and a rejection of the rationalizations and ideological creations of the old ruling class. It is the acceptance of the proletariat as the new ruling class and of the proletarian ideas as the ruling ideas.[45]

The rise of a revolutionary situation is based on the ripeness of the objective material conditions of production and the simultaneous readiness of subjective conditions found in the consciousness of the working class. "Subjective revolutionary ideas cannot catch hold without the objective conditions providing for a revolutionary class. Yet the objective conditions by themselves cannot create the revolutions until and unless working-class consciousness takes firm root."[46] Consciousness unfolds as material conditions affect workers and they collectively try to correct those conditions.

While a few respondents in this study do indeed have a conception of an alternative socialist society, it is often a vague notion of a more egalitarian system where workers have greater control over their lives. Perhaps the most sophisticated view is represented in the ideas expressed in an earlier chapter of some of the founders who are members of a socialist-feminist organization, New American Movement. It is important to note, however, that they did not found the organization as a radical movement in itself, and kept their own ideology relatively well-hidden. Therefore, there was no direct transmission of socialist ideas from founders to rank-and-file clerical workers. In fact, most of the early activists were careful not to express their political beliefs on the assumption that women office workers would not be receptive to them. There was clear intent to raise consciousness, but it was left to the office workers themselves to tie their own consciousness of their work problems to activism and to further developments of consciousness. That it was not in any way a socialist or radical organization in intent at a point in time almost three years after it was founded, attests to this direction their development has taken.

What has developed is an awareness of sets of shared objective conditions and collective actions, the intent of which is to remedy those conditions. Evidence for this has been given throughout the study. The organization at present combines the participants' sense of solidarity with these often militant actions, which results in greater solidarity and consciousness among members. Theoretically speaking, this combination of events may in fact lead to a more radical consciousness, though not necessarily.

Mann argues that without socialism as a base for action, the development of consciousness is limited. In the case of Baltimore Working Women, the base for action remains on the level of reforming the workplace, and that such reforms have to do specifically with problems faced by women workers. Yet, the uniqueness of the consciousness of these women office workers forces an examination of Marxist theories of consciousness. More specifically, if women workers are dissatisfied with their working conditions both as office workers and as women, and are willing to act collectively, this presents new conditions from which we must reconsider the development of consciousness.

It is clear that the women in this study saw connections between their work and family roles, the structure of the office and the role of patriarchy in the workplace, and the overall advantage both to capitalism and to individual male employers of hiring women in low-level positions. If we are to develop a theory of class consciousness that includes such awareness, then a conception of an alternative society must also include gender-specific consciousness.

The development of socialist-feminist theory speaks to the issue of gender-specific consciousness. If, in fact, the experiences of women under capitalism are uniquely tied to their family and sex-stereotyped social roles, then their consciousness of an alternative society would include creating a socialist society that focuses equally on the problem of sex inequalities. Sheila Rowbotham, an early proponent of socialist feminism, argues that the very situation of women under capitalism puts them in a unique position to conceive of an alternative society: "Simply because women have different expectations from men, simply because women have been kept out of certain areas of capitalism, they are well equipped to reach out to another form of social organization."[47] She explains further:

> The predicament of working-class women is the most potentially subversive to capitalism because it spans production and reproduction, class exploitation and sex oppression. The movement of working-class women is thus essential for the emergence of socialist feminism because the necessary connections are forced upon women who are working-class when they take action. When they occupy or strike they have their own conditioning as women, the attitude of husbands, the care of the family, the sexual patronage of union officials, the ridicule of the popular press . . . The overwhelming contempt from the middle class for their sex and their class. They are thus compelled to develop both sisterhood and solidarity or be crushed. They need each other. They need the support of male workers, and their fight at work connects immediately to their situation at home. Their organization and militancy is vital not only for women's liberation but for the whole socialist and working-class movement.[48]

Rowbotham makes a strong case for the potential development of a socialist-feminist movement in the working class. While a conception of this sort of movement in this particular study is minimal, there is considerable evidence that the consciousness of the respondents contains subjectively inseparable components of class and gender. From both theoretical and practical points of view, this is a significant finding if we are to understand the development of class consciousness for all workers. If there is a gender-specific consciousness for women, it undoubtedly exists for men as well. Men's consciousness about their expected family roles as tied to their work roles, the relationship of the male worker to authority and control at work, the expression of solidarity with other male workers, are all subjects in need of study. The type of job held by the worker is also significant in regards to the development of consciousness. The type of control to which workers are subject depends upon the job sector in which they work and elicits different types of dissatisfaction and expressions of solidarity. Given the sex-segregated nature of occupations, gender plays a part here, too.

The research carried out in this study only begins to examine the importance of gender in the development of consciousness. It is obviously limited by the selection of a highly specific population of activist women office workers. Further research into gender-specific consciousness will provide much needed insights into the prospects of consciousness and solidarity across gender and job sector lines.

NOTES

1. For further discussion of the class position of clerical workers, see Harry Braverman, *Labor and Monopoly Capital: The Degradation of Work in the Twentieth Century* (New York: Monthly Review Press, 1974); David Lockwood, *The Blackcoated Worker: A Study in Class Consciousness* (London: Ruskin House, George Allen and Unwin, Ltd., 1958); Stanley Aronowitz, *False Promises: The Shaping of America's Working Class Consciousness* (New York: McGraw-Hill, 1973); Gabriel Kolko, "Working Wives: Their Effects on the Structure of the Working Class," *Science and Society* 42 (1978):257–77; Richard Edwards, *Contested Terrain: The Transformation of the Workplace in the Twentieth Century.* (New York: Basic Books, 1979.)

2. Lockwood, *The Blackcoated Worker*, p. 15.

3. Edwards, *Contested Terrain*, p. 20.

4. Ibid., pp. 176–77.

5. Ibid., p. 178.

6. Elinor Langer, "The Women of the Telephone Company," *New York Review of Books* 14, nos. 5 and 6 (Boston, Mass.: The New England Free Press, reprinted pamphlet, 1970), pp. 19–20.

7. Sheila Rowbotham, *Woman's Consciousness, Man's World* (Middlesex, England: Penguin, 1973), pp. 83–84.

8. Edwards, *Contested Terrain*, p. 127; see also, Braverman, *Labor and Monopoly Capital*; Louise I. Arts, "Office Work, Office Technology and Women Office Workers." (Unpublished M.A. research paper, American University, 1979).

9. Edwards, *Contested Terrain*, p. 135.

10. Ibid., pp. 148–49.

11. Ibid., p. 147.

12. Ibid., p. 157.

13. Ibid., pp. 147–48.

14. Ibid., p. 153.

15. See Michael Mann, *Consciousness and Action Among the Western Working Class* (London: The Macmillan Press Ltd., 1980), pp. 20–23, 37; Aronowitz, *False Promises*, pp. 258–59.

16. Ibid., p. 260.

17. Kathy Bonk, "The Wage Gap," *National NOW Times*, August 1980, pp. 8–9.

18. Lillian Breslow Rubin, *Worlds of Pain: Life in Working-Class Families* (New York: Basic Books, 1976).

19. Ibid., p. 130.

20. Ibid., p. 55.

21. Ibid., pp. 168–69.

22. Ibid., pp. 174–75.

23. Ibid., p. 183.

24. Betty Robinson, "Women and Class Consciousness: A Proposal for the Dialectical Study of Class Consciousness," *The Insurgent Sociologist*, vol. VIII, no. IV (Winter 1979), p. 45.

25. Ibid., p. 47.

26. Ibid., p. 49.

27. Control over clerical work is discussed further in Edwards, *Contested Terrain*, pp. 88–89.

28. For a theoretical basis of class consciousness, the author used the following sources: Braverman, *Labor and Monopoly Capital*; Lockwood, *The Blackcoated Worker*; Gyorgy Lukcas, *History and Class Consciousness*, translated by Rodney Livingstone (Cambridge, Mass.: MIT Press, 1971); Mann, *Consciousness and Action Among the Western Working Class*; Wilhelm Reich, "What is Class Consciousness?" in Lee Baxandall (ed.) *Sex-Pol: Essays 1929–1934* (New York: Vintage Books, 1972).

29. Barbara Garson. *All the Livelong Day: The Meaning and Demeaning of Routine Work*. (New York: Doubleday, 1975); and Studs Terkel. *Working*. (New York: Pantheon, 1974).

30. Mann, *Consciousness and Action*, p. 13.

31. Ibid.

32. Rowbotham, *Woman's Consciousness*, p. 120.

33. Edwards, *Contested Terrain*, p. 205.

34. Annmarie Tröger, "The Coalition of Labor Union Women: Strategic Hope, Tactical Despair" in Rosalyn Baxandall, Linda Gordon, and Susan Reverby (eds.) *American Working Women: A Documentary History – 1600 to the Present* (New York: Vintage, 1976), p. 398.

35. Mann, *Consciousness and Action*, p. 13.

36. Ibid.

37. Langer, "The Women of the Telephone Company," pp. 21–22.

38. Rowbotham, *Women's Consciousness*, p. 95.

39. Robinson, "Women and Class Consciousness," p. 48.

40. Mann, *Consciousness and Action*, p. 19.

41. Gavin MacKenzie, *The Aristocracy of Labor: The Position of Skilled Craftsmen in the American Class Structure* (London: Cambridge University Press, 1973), p. 138; Braverman, *Labor and Monopoly Capital*, pp. 29–30; C. Wright Mills, *White Collar* (New York: Oxford University Press, 1951), p. 325.

42. Lockwood, *The Blackcoated Worker*, pp. 137–38; Charles H. Anderson, *The Political Economy of Social Class*. (Englewood Cliffs, N.J.: Prentice-Hall, 1974), p. 135.

43. Mann, *Consciousness and Action*, p. 13.

44. Ibid., p. 13.

45. Anderson, *The Political Economy*, p. 61.

46. Ibid., p. 61.

47. Rowbotham, *Woman's Consciousness*, pp. 101–2.

48. Ibid., p. 124.

Chapter 6

Conclusions: The Relationship between Dissatisfaction, Consciousness, and Action

The purpose of this study was to uncover the sources of dissatisfaction among an activist sector of women office workers and the types of consciousness and action that develop from that dissatisfaction. This has been pursued through several related avenues. An understanding of the historical development of the modern office and women's roles within it has provided the base from which work dissatisfaction was examined. An investigation of these dissatisfactions provided insight into the subjective experiences of a unique group of women workers, those who chose to work to improve working conditions for themselves and other women collectively. A comprehensive analysis of the types of consciousness developed among this group of women gives us insight both into their subjective world as well as filling in some important gaps in our theoretical understanding of consciousness. The limitations of this study both in terms of specific data collected as well as the overall nature of the data make it necessary to be somewhat speculative about the direct effects each of these have on one another. That is to say, it is difficult to measure the importance of various influences in people's lives leading to changes in consciousness. For instance, most respondents could say that the organization increased their consciousness in a general way, but the very nature of the dialectical process is one in which many factors interact on one another in such a complicated fashion that the effects are multiple and the dynamic is constant. Consequently, we cannot say categorically that a specific set of events led to a new level of consciousness that then led to participation in a given action. Nevertheless, we can observe a process that goes in a specific direction for the respondents and we can project theoretically that these factors affect one another in particular ways.

To best understand the findings of this study the following chart shows the path that is taken in the development of dissatisfaction, consciousness and action:

FIGURE 1

THE DEVELOPMENT OF DISSATISFACTION, CONSCIOUSNESS
AND ACTION

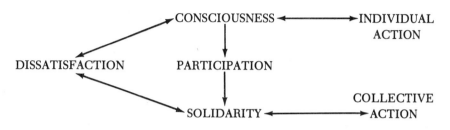

The multiple directions of the arrows indicate the dialectical nature of the relationship between these developmental process. Generally, we see that dissatisfaction leads to consciousness that leads to participation and solidarity and to both individual and collective action. As consciousness increases, so does participation, which further increases consciousness. Actions, too, have an effect of increasing participation. Participation leads to a sense of solidarity, which is also a type of consciousness, which then feeds back to increase dissatisfactions. Each step along this somewhat circular path will now be examined in greater depth.

DISSATISFACTION

Dissatisfaction is based on the conditions found in the office derived from its historical origins under capitalism and particularly its modern structures since the expansion and feminization of the office, and the technological changes leading to deskilling. Among the most important factors as described in the body of this research are the types of control used in the office. The interaction of these factors: growth of the office, the preponderance of women at the lowest levels, deskilling, and the interaction between a combination of simple, technical, and bureaucratic controls create a particular set of dynamics leading to discontent among the female office staff. These factors are inseparable in understanding why clerical workers are dissatisfied with their pay, promotions, lack of job titles and job postings, lack of job security, the routine and boring nature of their jobs, and lack of respect both for what they do and who they are. The work and the structure of the office have changed over time to the disadvantage of the clerk whose female status works to solidify her subordination within the framework of a stage of capitalism in which patriarchy still serves to control portions of the workforce and justifies exploitation of female workers.

Dissatisfaction is a dynamic force that needs an outlet. That some women have increased their consciousness, and acted to improve their working conditions, rather than accept those conditions or blame themselves for them, is a testimony to both new developments in an overall understanding of the purpose and potential of women's working life as well as the rise of publicly available outlets for airing dissatisfactions and correcting them. We must investigate this process further, as we see consciousness emerging from dissatisfaction.

CONSCIOUSNESS

The development of consciousness among the women in this study is a complex phenomenon. We have differentiated several types of consciousness that can be separated for the purposes of discussion, but are, in fact, inexorably tied together. Theoretically a person's consciousness grows from simple to complex, with ever-increasing knowledge about the causes of dissatisfaction and with whom one shares such discontent. This study has differentiated several interrelated types of consciousness that can be broken down into two levels for the purposes of discussion. The first level consists of job consciousness and feminist consciousness that have been found to interact so closely that it might be a distortion to separate them. One of the most significant findings of this research is the consistent link women office workers make between their working life and their status as women, particularly within the family. That these two factors are so closely tied indicates a type of consciousness heretofore unrecognized either theoretically or pragmatically. This is not surprising, given the tradition of Marxist studies of work and workers' consciousness and the efforts to organize labor. Traditionally, the male industrial workforce has been considered the proper subject for study, and the worker most important to organize.

It is here that we must recognize the impact of patriarchy as a structural condition within modern capitalism, for it is the objective conditions of these workers, who, both as women and as clerical workers, share a subjective reality. While this has certainly worked to the disadvantage of women and to the advantage of male employers, both as individuals and as entire companies, it has also placed women office workers in a unique position from which to develop higher stages of consciousness. It had been argued that the most alienated workers are not the ones who are likely to become class conscious. Rather, it is those who can link various portions of their lives, particularly their work and family experiences, into an integrated process, in which they have an impact on each other. Women, because of their traditional family roles and their present position in the workforce, often having to take full responsibilities in both realms, find the relationship between the two inseparable. Thus their potential for developing class consciousness, the second level of consciousness discussed in this research, is higher than for those whose lives are not influenced in this way.

From the first level of job consciousness and feminist consciousness, the respondents in this study derived an interest in sharing job-related problems with others and planning ways to improve working conditions. It is at this point that we begin to see the complexity of the interactions between consciousness, participation, solidarity, and action. There is a constant flow among these processes; as consciousness increases, participation increases, as does solidarity and activism. As these increase, they raise the level of consciousness, and so back and forth, building upon each other. The process moves in an ever-increasing development of consciousness and its expression through action and solidarity.

The second level of consciousness, class consciousness, develops in the context of the increased participation, solidarity, and action taken by the members of this working women's organization. Before discussing class consciousness, we will examine each of these factors.

Participation

The decision to join with others who experience similar life situations is a decision to view the individual as part of a social whole rather than as an individual alone, and is the first step in acting upon one's consciousness. More specifically, to participate in an organization with other women office workers who are dissatisfied with working conditions indicates that such activities are a positive step and preferable to coping alone. Evidence of this is found in the body of this research in which respondents discuss the advantages of belonging to this group, both from the standpoint of solidarity with other working women as well as from the expectation of accomplishing specific goals through deliberate action. What makes participation in this case even more significant is the limited experience of collective participation historically among either women or clericals. The reasons for this change have already been discussed, and we must recognize the effects of the new conditions of the office and of women that have given rise to the likelihood of participation among women clericals.

Solidarity

Solidarity emerges with the combined growth of consciousness and participation. While participation is the active joining of an organization or other collective effort, solidarity is the recognition of both shared experiences and the need for joining together to confront and resolve common problems. It is an attitude that reflects growing consciousness and is, in fact, an important component of consciousness itself. It also follows from participation in a group collectively, as the opportunity to discuss common problems increases with the presence of a forum for such discussion. As these three experiences reinforce one another positively, all tend to grow proportionately. The solidarity that emerges is significantly specific to women office workers. The relief and strength that are expressed when feelings of solidarity develop is considerable and indicates the difficulty in developing solidarity in other contexts, such as the workplace or in one's own family or friendship group. There is also widespread recognition that participation and solidarity create a situation where action is realizable.

Action

As the chart indicates, action can take place in two possible ways: as an individual or collective effort. Individual action results from dissatisfaction and a certain amount of consciousness that the cause of the discontent may be confronted. Participation does not play a role in this case. Such action can come in a variety of forms: quitting one's job to find more satisfactory work; asserting oneself in order to demand higher pay, promotion, or other improvements in working conditions; receiving training or education to increase the possibility of advancement; or, sabotage of the mechanics of work or the relations between the employer and worker. Individual actions occur with great regularity and may result in success for individual women, though the risk of failure, and in some cases punishment, is high. Furthermore, the extent to which individual actions are successful is limited to the specific context in which they are performed. That is to say, a woman who asks for a raise can succeed only if it is already a possibility within the context of the particular workplace (given the structure of her office, willingness and power of her boss to give her a raise, and so on), and that act certainly does not ensure the potential for future raises. By the same token, a worker who sabotages equipment succeeds only until the machine is repaired. The degree of power acquired in these cases is minimal and shortlived, and in and of itself does not question the structure of the office or relative power of employers and their treatment of their employees. Nevertheless, for individual workers it may develop into improved working conditions, or at least some relief from drudgery. It may also serve as an example to other workers, which increases the potential for collective action.

If actions are taken collectively, the results may be quite different. The most obvious difference is in the number of people who are acting and for whom the actions are taken. In the case of Baltimore Working Women, the two groups are not necessarily the same. In fact, this brings out a crucial aspect of the importance of participation and solidarity to the organization. It has already been pointed out that the actions are taken for the purpose of improving working conditions in the most female-dominated areas. Zeroing in on a bank's job-posting policy may not affect individual members of the organization at all. But it will affect all the clerical workers in that bank and possibly those in other banks whose management changes policy to avoid confrontation. The willingness of BWW members to support such action can only arise out of a consciousness of the advantages of collective action and solidarity with those who share similar circumstances. This research has reported approval of such actions based on generalized interest in helping women office workers, regardless of the self-interest of individual members.

Furthermore, respondents reported that collective action increases their sense of solidarity with other members of the organization, providing them with a context of strength from which they can challenge the power of corporations and banks. In addition, such actions and solidarity give individual women courage to confront their job problems as individuals, thus encouraging improvement of their particular situation. Once again, we see a circular relationship between consciousness, participation, action, and solidarity.

All of these elements interact upon each other giving rise to ever-increasing consciousness. Yet, actions are based almost entirely on accepting the basic power dynamics of the workplace — the right of employers to hire, fire, and promote workers. Actions taken are in the context of working within the office structure as it exists. None explicitly calls for a reorganization of power or questions the capitalist mode of production and control. The focus of action is found in the implementation of increased rights and respect for workers. The implications for development of a program that raises such questions of production and control may be inherent in this sort of protest action. The actions themselves do not necessarily move in that direction, nor does consciousness, though increasing, necessarily evolve into demands for structural change in the context of a more radical consciousness. With increases in participation, solidarity, and action, we see some changes in consciousness at the second level, class consciousness.

CLASS CONSCIOUSNESS

Class consciousness was examined using Mann's framework of development from class identity to class opposition to class totality to a conception of an alternative society. Mann himself points out that these concepts are both closely related as well as developed somewhat independently. For instance, class opposition may be stronger at some points than class identity, in spite of the logic of moving from identity to opposition. Development of class consciousness is uneven depending upon the historical context, the structure of the workplace, and, in the case of this study, the gender of the worker. In fact, this research found that among respondents, class identity and class opposition were strong, encompassing a gender-specific consciousness of women workers. Again, this is influenced by the patriarchal structure of the office and society in general and the traditional sex role expectations of women in the workplace and the family.

Class identity involves a step beyond job and feminist consciousness to an identity with others who share the same class as the respondent, regardless of gender or occupation. Strong identity with other working women, both in and out of the clerical field, was evident. Identity with male workers was less strong. This was not surprising given the strength of gender-identity among the respondents, clearly among the most important subjective experiences they have. Obviously workers identify closest with those who share their positions, and the lack of identity with male workers exemplifies the uniqueness of the position and experiences of women workers. It was argued in the body of this paper that gender-specific identity does not in itself interfere with increasing identity with all workers regardless of gender, but rather is one important aspect of class identity found among women workers. Men, by the same token, undoubtedly experience their own form of gender-specific class identity, rarely regarding women clericals as fellow travelers. To tie these two forms of identity into a shared and complimentary identity is the work of labor organizers who wish to increase class consciousness and solidarity among both women and men.

Similarly, class opposition also takes on gender-specific characteristics, acknowledging the sex-based division of labor between female clerks and male management. An important observation here is that opposition to men among respondents is found only in the context of men as bosses or controlling husbands — that is, men in positions of power. Men in general are not seen as enemies, but it is assumed that men, given their higher status and greater power, are more likely to be in a position to supervise women workers, and thus to have class interests in opposition to those of women clerical workers. This notion indicates that while gender is an important component of oppression for women clericals, it is seen in the context of power inequities based primarily on class differences.

Class totality represents the ability of the worker to combine class identity and class opposition to a larger sense of class relations. Operationalizing this concept was difficult, for it is theoretically abstract, as Mann points out. The only data available in this study that indicates any relationship here was the respondents' opinions of labor unions. This was used on the assumption that approval of unions in general represented a more advanced stage of class identity encompassing a recognition of the need to organize among other members of the same class in opposition to management. Further, it indicates a consciousness concerning organizing in a variety of workplaces, in addition to the office.

Respondents had mixed feelings about unions. A few were union members. The majority approved of them as the major institution through which goals could be accomplished. But even with this approval, reservations were expressed on several counts. Fear of domination by male leadership and the subsequent lessening of importance of women's issues was a specific concern. On a more general level there was suspicion of the intentions of large labor unions. Throughout, there were strong feelings that unions are useful to a certain degree, but attention to women's issues required something more than unions could offer. A few respondents expressed a fairly strong dislike of unions and hoped the organization would not affiliate with any, but rather would pressure unions from the outside to pay attention to women's issues. Again we see a gender-specific consciousness prevailing, and while there is general interest in aligning with other workers, particularly women in other occupations and working men, it is with some caution that this is suggested. The awareness that women's needs often do not get addressed by unions discourages tacit approval of unionizing.

The last and most advanced stage of class consciousness, the conception of an alternative society, is the least prevalent of the types of consciousness examined. This finding is not surprising given the overall experiences of the working class, the labor movement, and the general attitudes toward socialism in this country. In fact, it would be surprising if there were development of this stage to any large degree. Few respondents envisioned a different economic system than capitalism nor did they speculate about alternatives to workplace structure that might be more democratically organized or socialistic. A small number expressed these ideas in a vague way, but offered no specific goals for the reorganization of society. Nevertheless, it is useful to speculate what this stage might be like if we carry through what we have learned about the development of consciousness so far. It is evident that we could expect gender-specific ideas to prevail in this conception of an alternative society.

Socialist feminists have made it their task to argue for an alternative society that incorporates feminist principles in any notion of revolutionary social change. The inclusion of the concept of patriarchy in the context of capitalism broadens our knowledge of the experience of both female and male workers. The attention given to family issues by socialist feminists reflects the very experiences of the respondents in this study. As has been pointed out, a number of founders of this working women's organization describe themselves as socialist feminists. They are in essentially the same position in this movement as the male left is in in the labor movement, having a more specific conception of an alternative society than do the rank and file of that movement.

The remaining question is whether we can expect a strengthening of this concept among the rank and file. Consciousness develops, but does it threaten the structural base of the workplace or the economy as a whole? So far in the United States, while there is considerable fluctuation in consciousness at different points in economic development, there is little evidence that there has been any serious challenge to capitalism on the part of the working class. It has been argued that the uniqueness of the U.S. labor force, with its mobility (based in ideology more than reality), and its racial and sexual divisions, has served to control class consciousness and action. American Marxists question the timing of the confluence of objective and subjective conditions that are expected to give rise to revolution. They have been criticized for not paying attention to the working class and misinterpreting its consciousness. This is particularly true of women workers and white-collar workers neither of whom, until recently, have been given much serious attention as members of the working class. Yet, given the evidence of this study concerning both the consciousness of this group of workers as well as the structural conditions, a strong argument could be made to look here for great increases in class consciousness. The uniqueness of the position of women clerical workers is that they are oppressed by both capitalism and patriarchy, which at critical times are faced with challenge and, in fact, challenge each other. The inevitability of the conflicts inherent in this relationship and the increasing opportunities to challenge power through collective groups encourages growth in consciousness. The effect of the women's movement is particularly instrumental in these circumstances, for as the ideology of sexism is challenged in personal and public life (that is, in the family and the workplace) and women begin to see avenues for self-development opening to them, their dissatisfactions with their current status will grow. At the same time, organized groups become available to encourage the raising of consciousness and solidarity, and call for militant action. As we have seen, the subjective experience of consciousness ties the personal and public worlds. This is a reflection of the objective conditions that require women to fulfill the needs of both capitalism and patriarchy at a time when it is getting more difficult to do so. The raising of consciousness in this context is an embodiment of the contradictory expectations that both free women and tie them down at the same time. In classic dialectical fashion, we can expect these women to try to resolve these conflicts, leading them to increased action and higher stages of consciousness. We still cannot definitively answer the question as to the potential for revolutionary consciousness for this particular group of workers. What we can say is that there is growing interest among this group to improve working conditions and particularly to gain more control over their working life. The attention given to issues concerning work relations — respect, in particular — indicates a strong desire to have greater control over one's work experience. If it is determined that this cannot be accomplished satisfactorily within the structure of the workplace as it now exists, we will have a better idea of the direction the development of consciousness will take. As for now, those with the most advanced consciousness are calling for structural reforms. It will be interesting to watch the continuing dialectical process between capitalism, reform, consciousness, and action as more working women challenge their place in the workforce. Clearly, there will be an increase in confrontations, as employers begin to take the challenges to their power more seriously, particularly as the workplace itself adjusts to new types of control as the office grows and becomes more technologically sophisticated.

THEORETICAL AND PRACTICAL IMPLICATIONS
OF THE RESEARCH

Implicit in this analysis is the suggestion that we must closely examine gender-specific consciousness in both women and men as significant aspects of class consciousness. This is problematic since so much of what has been taken to be indicative of class consciousness is, in fact, male-specific class consciousness. Nevertheless, if the working class as a whole is ever to have solidarity across gender lines, we must first understand consciousness that is derived from different gender experiences, both in the workplace and in the family. This means for men as well as women the relationship of home life to work life must be thoroughly studied. Patriarchy, as it affects the entire labor force at work and in personal lives, is an important area needing further attention. At present, theories of class consciousness are limited by ignoring gender as an important contributing factor.

In a more practical vein, organizing the workplace takes on new characteristics when attending to the world of women in the office. Organized labor periodically tries to organize women workers, and this is successful to one degree or another. Few have bothered to orient organizing strategies to the special interests, needs, and problems of women, especially those found in offices, as opposed to industry, where unions are already familiar to workers. Without knowledge of the life experiences of women who work a double day, who experience a particular form of exploitation as women, who must adjust to the expansion of the office and the deskilling of the work, organizing is likely to remain limited to a small segment of this sector of the workforce. The labor movement could learn from working women's organizations how to attract membership, involve workers, increase their consciousness, create leadership from the rank and file, and promote actions that raise issues and question the relationship between employer and employee.

The fact that women office workers are organizing enthusiastically in record numbers is testimony to their readiness for collective action under the right conditions. The historical disinterest, and in some cases, outright antagonism of labor unions toward women workers prevented this from happening in the past, and encouraged divisions within the working class favorable to both capitalism and patriarchy. Given the increase of office workers in the economy, it is now in the interest of unions to try to organize this sector of the labor force. Without attention paid to specific women's issues, this could easily fail.

Bibliography

Anderson, Charles H. *The Political Economy of Social Class*. Englewood Cliffs, N.J.: Prentice-Hall, 1974.

Aronowitz, Stanley. *False Promises: The Shaping of America's Working Class Consciousness*. New York: McGraw-Hill, 1973.

Arts, Louise I. "Office Work, Office Technology and Women Office Workers." Unpublished M.A. research paper, American University, 1979.

Bain, George Sayers. *The Growth of White-Collar Unionism*. London: Oxford University Press, 1970.

Baker, Sally Hillsman. "Women in Blue-Collar and Service Occupations." In *Women Working: Theories and Facts in Perspective*, edited by Ann H. Stromberg and Shirley Harkess, pp. 339–376. Palo Alto, California: Mayfield, 1978.

Baxandall, Rosalyn; Linda Gordon; and Susan Reverby, eds. *America's Working Women: A Documentary History – 1600 to the Present*. New York: Vintage, 1976.

Bell, Carolyn Shaw. "Women and Work: An Economic Appraisal." In *Women Working: Theories and Facts in Perspective*, edited by Ann H. Stromberg and Shirley Harkess, pp. 10–28. Palo Alto, California: Mayfield, 1978.

Benet, Mary Kathleen. *Secretary: Enquiry into the Female Ghetto*. London: Sedgwick and Jackson, 1972.

Benston, Margaret. "The Political Economy of Women's Liberation." *Monthly Review* (September 1969):13–25.

Blake, Judith. "The Changing Status of Women in Developing Countries." *Scientific American* (September 1974):137–47.

Blau, Francine D. "The Data on Women Workers, Past, Present, and Future." In *Women Working: Theories and Facts in Perspective*, edited by Ann H. Stromberg and Shirley Harkess, pp. 29–62. Palo Alto, California: Mayfield, 1978.

Blaxall, Martha and Barbara Reagan, eds. *Women and the Workplace: The Implications of Occupational Segregation*. Chicago: The University of Chicago Press, 1976.

Blum, Albert A.; Martin Estey; James W. Kuhn; Wesley A. Wildman; and Leo Troy. *White-Collar Workers*. New York: Random House, 1971.

Bonk, Kathy. "The Wage Gap," *National NOW Times* (August 1980):8–9.

Braverman, Harry. *Labor and Monopoly Capital: The Degradation of Work in the Twentieth Century*. New York: Monthly Review Press, 1974.

Brownlee, W. Elliot, and Mary M. Brownlee. *Women in the American Economy: A Documentary History, 1675 to 1929*. New Haven: Yale University Press, 1976.

Bularzik, Mary. "Sexual Harassment at the Workplace," *Radical America* 12 (1978):25–43.

Cole, Stephan. *The Unionization of Teachers: A Case Study of the UFT*. New York: Praeger, 1969.

Crozier, Michel. *The World of the Office Worker*. Chicago: The University of Chicago Press, 1971.

Daniels, Arlene Kaplan. "Feminist Perspectives in Sociological Research." In *Another Voice: Feminist Perspectives on Social Life and Social Science*, edited by Marcia Millman and Rosabeth Moss Kanter, pp. 340–80. New York: Anchor, 1975.

Davies, Margery. "Women's Place is at the Typewriter: The Feminization of the Clerical Labor Force," *Radical America*, vol. 8, no. 4 (July–August 1974): 1–28.

Davies, Margery and Michael Reich. "On the Relationship Between Sexism and Capitalism." In *The Capitalist System: A Radical Analysis of American Society*, edited by Richard C. Edwards, Michael Reich and Thomas E. Weisskopf, pp. 348–56. Englewood Cliffs, N.J.: Prentice-Hall, 1972.

Drier, Peter. "Raises Not Roses: Organizing in the Sexual Ghetto," *In These Times* (June 13–19, 1979):12–13.

Dye, Nancy Schrom. "Feminism or Unionism? The New York Women's Trade Union League and the Labor Movement," *Feminist Studies* 3 (1975):111–25.

Edwards, Richard. *Contested Terrain: The Transformation of the Workplace in the Twentieth Century*. New York: Basic Books, 1979.

Eisenstein, Zillah. "Developing a Theory of Capitalist Patriarchy and Socialist Feminism." In *Capitalist Patriarchy and the Case for Socialist Feminism*, edited by Zillah Eisenstein, pp. 5–40. London: Monthly Review Press, 1979.

————, "The State, the Patriarchal Family and Working Mothers," *Kapitalistate: Working Papers on the Capitalist State*, no. 8 (1980):43–66.

Ellinger, Mickey and John Rowntree. "More on the Political Economy of Women's Liberation," *Monthly Review* (January 1970):26–32. Reprinted pamphlet. *The Political Economy of Women's Liberation*. San Francisco: United Front Press, pp. 16–22.

Feldberg, Roslyn L. and Evelyn Nakano Glenn. "Male and Female: Job Versus Gender Models in the Sociology of Work," *Social Problems* 26 (1979):524–38.

Friedan, Betty. *The Feminine Mystique*. New York: Dell, 1963.

Garson, Barbara. *All the Livelong Day: The Meaning and Demeaning of Routine Work*. New York: Doubleday, 1975.

Glaser, Barney G. and Anselm L. Strauss. *The Discovery of Grounded Theory: Strategies for Qualitative Research*. Chicago: Aldine, 1967.

Glenn, Evelyn Nakano and Roslyn L. Feldberg. "Clerical Work: The Female Occupation." In *Women: A Feminist Perspective*, 2nd edition, edited by Jo Freeman, pp. 313–38. Palo Alto, California: Mayfield, 1979.

Goldberg, Marilyn Power. "The Economic Exploitation of Women." In *The Capitalist System: A Radical Analysis of American Society*, edited by Richard C. Edwards, Michael Reich and Thomas E. Weisskopf, pp. 341–48. Englewood Cliffs, N.J.: Prentice-Hall, 1972.

Grandjean, Burke D. and Patricia A. Taylor. "Job Satisfaction Among Female Clerical Workers: 'Status Panic' or the Opportunity Structure of Office Work?", *Sociology of Work and Occupations* vol. 7, no. 1 (February 1980): 33–53.

Hacker, Sally L. "Sex Stratification, Technology and Organizational Change: A Longitudinal Case Study of A. T. and T." *Social Problems*, vol. 26, no. 5 (June 1979):539–57.

Hartmann, Heidi. "Capitalism, Patriarchy, and Job Segregation by Sex," *Signs: Journal of Women in Culture and Society*, vol. 1, no. 3, Part 2 (Spring 1976): 137–69.

Hoos, Ida R. "When the Computer Takes Over the Office," *Harvard Business Review* (July–August 1960):102–12.

Howe, Louise Kapp. *Pink Collar Workers: Inside the World of Women's Work*. New York: Avon, 1978.

Jacoby, Robin. "The Women's Trade Union League and American Feminism," *Feminist Studies* 3, nos. 1/2 (1975):126–40.

Kanter, Rosabeth Moss. "Women and the Structure of Organizations: Explorations in Theory and Behavior." In *Another Voice: Feminist Perspectives on Social Life and Social Science*, edited by Marcia Millman and Rosabeth Moss Kanter, pp. 34–74. New York: Anchor, 1975.

Kassalow, Everett M. "White-Collar Unionism in the United States." In *White-Collar Trade Unions: Contemporary Developments in Industrialized Societies*, edited by Adolf Sturmthal, pp. 305–64. Chicago: University of Illinois Press, 1967.

Kessler-Harris, Alice. "Where Are the Organized Women Workers?", *Feminist Studies* 3, nos. 1/2 (1975):92–110.

Kolko, Gabriel. "Working Wives: Their Effects on the Structure of the Working Class," *Science and Society* 42 (1978):257–77.

Kornhauser, Arthur; Harold L. Sheppard; and Albert J. Mayer. *When Labor Votes: A Study of Auto Workers*. New York: University Books, 1956.

Kusterer, Ken C. *Know-How on the Job: The Important Working Knowledge of "Unskilled" Workers*. Boulder, Colorado: Westview Press, 1978.

Langer, Elinor. "The Women of the Telephone Company." *New York Review of Books* 14, nos 5 and 6, reprinted pamphlet. Boston, Massachusetts: New England Free Press, 1970.

LeGrande, Linda H. "Women in Labor Organizations: Their Ranks are Increasing," *Monthly Labor Review* 101 (1978):8–14.

Levinson, Andrew. *The Working-Class Majority*. New York: Penguin, 1974.

Lockwood, David. *The Blackcoated Worker: A Study in Class Consciousness*. London: Ruskin House, George Allen and Unwin, Ltd., 1958.

Lofland, John. *Analyzing Social Settings: A Guide to Qualitative Observation and Analysis*. Belmont, California: Wadsworth, 1971.

Lorber, Judith. "Trust, Loyalty, and the Place of Women in the Informal Organization of Work." In *Women: A Feminist Perspective*, 2nd edition, edited by Jo Freeman, pp. 371–381. Palo Alto, California: Mayfield, 1979.

Lukcas, Gyorgy, *History and Class Consciousness*. Translated by Rodney Livingstone. Cambridge, Massachusetts: MIT Press, 1971.

McCall, George J. and J. L. Simmons, eds. *Issues in Participant Observation: A Test and Reader*. Reading, Massachusetts: Addison-Wesley, 1969.

McCourt, Kathleen. *Working-Class Women and Grass Roots Politics.* Bloomington: Indiana University Press, 1977.

MacKenzie, Gavin. *The Aristocracy of Labor: The Position of Skilled Craftsmen in the American Class Structure.* London: Cambridge University Press, 1973.

Mann, Michael. *Consciousness and Action Among the Western Working Class.* London: The Macmillan Press, Ltd. 1980.

Maupin, Joyce. *Working Women and their Organizations – 150 Years of Struggle.* Berkeley, California: Union Wage Educational Committee, 1974.

Milkman, Ruth. "Organizing the Sexual Division of Labor: Historical Perspectives on 'Women's Work' and the American Labor Movement," *Socialist Review,* No. 49 (April 1980):95–150.

Miller, Joanne. "Individual and Occupational Determinants of Job Satisfaction: A Focus on Gender Differences," *Sociology of Work and Occupations,* vol. 7, no. 3 (August 1980):337–66.

Millman, Marcia and Rosabeth Moss Kanter, eds. *Another Voice: Feminist Perspectives on Social Life and Social Science.* New York: Anchor, 1975.

Mills, C. Wright. *White Collar.* New York: Oxford University Press, 1951.

Mitchell, Juliet. *Women's Estate.* New York: Vintage, 1973.

Olesen, Virginia L. and Frances Katsuranis. "Urban Nomads: Women in Temporary Clerical Services." In *Women Working: Theories and Facts in Perspective,* edited by Ann H. Stromberg and Shirley Harkess, pp. 316–38. Palo Alto, California: Mayfield, 1978.

Ollman, Bertell. *Social and Sexual Revolution: Essays on Marx and Reich.* Boston: South End Press, 1979.

Oppenheimer, Valerie Kincade. *The Female Labor Force in the United States: Demographic and Economic Factors Governing its Growth and Changing Composition.* Westport, Connecticut: Greenwood Press, 1970.

O'Sullivan, Judith and Rosemary Gallick. *Workers and Allies: Female Participation in the American Trade Union Movement, 1824–1976.* Washington, D.C.: Smithsonian Institution Press, 1975.

Palmer, Phyllis Marynick and Sharon Lee Grant. *The Status of Clerical Workers: A Summary Analysis of Research Findings and Trends.* Washington, D.C.: Women's Studies Program, George Washington University, Business and Professional Women's Foundation, 1979.

Peck, Sidney M. *The Rank and File Leader*. New Haven, Connecticut: College and University Press, 1963.

————. "Fifty Years After a Theory of the Labor Movement: Class Conflict in the United States," *The Insurgent Sociologist* 8, nos. 2 and 3 (1978):4–13.

Perlman, Mark. *Labor Union Theories in America: Background and Development*. Evanston, Illinois: Row, Peterson and Co., 1958.

Perlman, Selig. *A Theory of the Labor Movement*. New York: Augustus M. Kelley, 1949. (Originally published 1928.)

Raphael, Edna E. "Working Women and Their Membership in Labor Unions," *Monthly Labor Review* 97 (1974):27–33.

Reich, Wilhelm. "What is Class Consciousness?" (Originally published 1934.) In *Sex-Pol: Essays, 1929–1934*, edited by Lee Baxandall, pp. 275–358. New York: Vintage, 1972.

Robinson, Betty. "Women and Class Consciousness: A Proposal for the Dialectical Study of Class Consciousness," *The Insurgent Sociologist*, 8, no. 4 (Winter 1979):44–51.

Roby, Pamela. "Sociology and Women in Working-Class Jobs." In *Another Voice: Feminist Perspectives on Social Life and Social Science*, edited by Marcia Millman and Rosabeth Moss Kanter, pp. 203–39. New York: Anchor, 1975.

Rowbotham, Sheila. *Woman's Consciousness, Man's World*. Middlesex, England: Penguin, 1973.

Rubin, Lillian Breslow. *Worlds of Pain: Life in Working Class Families*. New York: Basic Books, 1976.

Sexton, Patricia Cayo. "Workers (Female) Arise! On Founding the Coalition of Labor Union Women," *Dissent* 21 (1974):380–95.

Sikula, Andrew F. "The Uniqueness of Secretaries as Employees," *Journal of Business Education* 48 (February 1973):203–5.

Smuts, Robert W. *Women and Work in America*. New York: Schocken Books, 1976. (Originally published New York: Columbia University Press, 1959.)

Strauss, Anselm, *et. al.* "The Process of Field Work." In *Issues in Participant Observation: A Text and Reader*, edited by George J. McCall and J. L. Simmons, pp. 24–27. Reading, Massachusetts: Addison-Wesley, 1969.

Stromberg, Ann H. and Shirley Harkess, eds. *Women Working: Theories and Facts in Perspective*. Palo Alto, California: Mayfield, 1978.

Sturmthal, Adolf, ed. *White-Collar Trade Unions: Contemporary Developments in Industrialized Societies.* Chicago, University of Illinois Press, 1967.

Tepperman, Jean. *Not Servants, Not Machines: Office Workers Speak Out.* Boston: Beacon Press, 1976.

Terkel, Studs. *Working.* New York: Pantheon, 1974.

Tilly, Charles. *From Mobilization to Revolution.* Reading, Mass.: Addison-Wesley, 1978.

Tröger, Annemarie. "The Coalition of Labor Union Women: Strategic Hope, Tactical Despair." In *America's Working Women: A Documentary History — 1600 to the Present*, edited by Rosalyn Baxandall, *et al.*, pp. 390–99. New York: Vintage, 1976.

Tucker, Robert C., ed. *The Marx-Engels Reader.* New York: W. W. Norton, 1972.

U.S. Department of Commerce, Bureau of the Census. *Historical Statistics of the United States: Colonial Times to 1970.* Washington, D.C.: Government Printing Office, 1975.

U.S. Department of Commerce, Bureau of the Census. *Statistical Abstract of the United States, 1980*, 101st edition. Washington, D.C.: Government Printing Office, 1980.

U.S. Department of Labor, Bureau of Labor Statistics. *U.S. Working Women: A Databook.* Washington, D.C.: Government Printing Office Bulletin, 1977.

Vogel, Alfred. "Your Clerical Workers Are Ripe for Unionism." In *America's Working Women: A Documentary History — 1600 to the Present*, edited by Rosalyn Baxandall *et al.*, pp. 351–53. New York: Vintage, 1976.

Wagner, David. "Clerical Workers: How 'Unorganizable' Are They?" *Labor Center Review*, 2, no. 1 (Spring/Summer 1979):20–50.

Wertheimer, Barbara M. "Union is Power: Sketches from Women's Labor History." In *Women: A Feminist Perspective*, edited by Jo Freeman, pp. 339–70. Palo Alto, California: Mayfield, 1979.

————. *We Were There: The Story of Working Women in America.* New York: Pantheon, 1977.

Women Employed in Baltimore. *Women Employed: Analysis of the Employment Situation of Women Working In Baltimore Offices.* Baltimore, Maryland: Women Employed in Baltimore, 1978.

Women's Work Project, The. *Women Organizing the Office.* New York: A Union for Radical Political Economics Political Education Project, 1978.

Working Women, National Association of Office Workers. *The Bill of Rights for Women Office Workers.* Cleveland, Ohio: Working Women, National Association of Office Workers. Unpublished pamphlet.

Working Women, National Association of Office Workers. *Vanished Dreams: Age Discrimination and the Older Woman Worker.* Cleveland, Ohio: Working Women, National Association of Office Workers, August, 1980.

Zaretsky, Eli. *Capitalism, the Family and Personal Life.* New York: Harper Colophon, 1976.

Zelditch, Morris Jr. "Some Methodological Problems of Field Studies." In *Issues in Participant Observation: A Text and Reader*, edited by George J. McCall and J. L. Simmons, pp. 5–19. Reading, Mass.: Addison-Wesley, 1969.

Index

actions, 38, 43, 92, 109, 120, 130–31, 133, 134–35, 138–39, 140; collective, 126, 130–31, 134, 135; individual, 92, 130, 134–35 (*see also* Baltimore Working Women: actions)

activism, 22, 88, 89, 90, 91, 92, 95, 109, 121, 133

AFL, 17, 122 (*see also* organized labor, unions)

age, 41

age discrimination, 39, 40–41, 46, 52–53 (*see also* older working women)

alternative society, conception of, 109, 124–27, 136, 137–39

altruism, 48–49, 91

Anderson, Charles, 125

Aronowitz, Stanley, 3

Baltimore Working Women (BWW), 1, 34, 35–58, 72, 96, 98, 100, 101, 109–10, 123, 126, 135; actions, 38, 50, 51–53, 54; campaigns, 43, 45, 52–53, 54, 57; committees, 38, 43, 45, 46, 50–51, 56; funding, 35, 38, 39, 44, 50, 51; goals, 38–41, 46, 52–53, 133; history, 35–37; meetings, 38, 41, 43, 45–46, 47–48, 50, 57; membership, 35, 38, 40, 41–44, 47–49, 50–51, 53, 54, 67, 76, 110–11, 115, 116–17, 119; officers, 37, 43, 44, 46, 50, 51, 57; personal development, 54–58; power structure, 50–51; recruitment, 44; staff, 35, 36, 37, 42–43, 44, 45, 46, 47, 50, 51, 57; structure, 41–43 (*see also* actions)

banking, 34, 39, 46, 51, 52, 69, 70, 91, 111, 113–14, 117, 135

blue-collar work, 19, 21, 22–23, 59, 64 (*see also* industrial labor)

Braverman, Harry, 3

bureaucracy, 12, 29, 81, 84–85, 86, 87–88, 103

capitalism, 3, 11, 13–14, 16, 25, 27, 29, 82–83, 87, 92, 93, 102, 109, 112–13, 114, 122, 123–24, 126–27, 131–32, 135, 137–39, 140 (*see also* patriarchal capitalism)

children, 23, 26, 27, 41, 60, 61, 62–63, 68, 103, 104, 105–106

CIO, 17 (*see also* organized labor, unions)

Civil War, 14

class, 11, 19, 28, 64, 79, 92, 99, 102, 108–109, 111, 112–13, 118, 124, 127, 136–37 (*see also* middle-class women, working class, working-class women)

class conflict, 125

class consciousness, 2, 79–80, 82, 84, 88, 97, 102, 108–28, 132–33, 135–40 (*see also* alternative society, class identity, class opposition, class totality)

class identity, 87, 109, 110–13, 136, 137

class opposition, 109, 113–18, 136, 137

class totality, 109, 118–25, 136, 137

clerical workers (*see* male office workers, office work, women office workers)

Coalition of Labor Union Women, 28

confidence, 54–56, 101

confidentiality, 6, 7–8

consciousness, 1, 2–3, 26, 28, 51, 52–53, 79–128, 130–33, 135; among men, 127; relationship between job consciousness and feminist consciousness, 102–108 (*see also* class consciousness, feminist consciousness, job consciousness)

consumerism, 23, 24, 60

About the Author

ROBERTA GOLDBERG is Assistant Professor of Sociology at the University of Pittsburgh at Bradford in Bradford, Pennsylvania. Her areas of interest include sociology of the workplace, the family, and sex roles. Dr. Goldberg holds a Ph.D. from American University, Washington, D.C.